^{THE} EGYPTIAN
ᗞᗞ BOOK OF ᗞᗞ
LIVING AND DYING

THE EGYPTIAN
BOOK OF
LIVING AND DYING

JOANN FLETCHER

Thorsons
Directions for Life

The Egyptian Book of Living and Dying
Joann Fletcher

Thorsons
An imprint of HarperCollins*Publishers*
77–85 Fulham Palace Road
Hammersmith, London, England W6 8JB

Published in the United States by Thorsons in 2002

Conceived, created and designed by
Duncan Baird Publishers
6th Floor, Castle House
75–76 Wells Street
London W1T 3QH

Project Editor: Peter Bently
Designer: Dan Sturges
Picture Editor: Cecilia Weston-Baker
Commissioned Artwork: Sally Taylor (artistpartners ltd)

Managing Editor: Christopher Westhorp
Managing Designer: Manisha Patel

Library of Congress Cataloging-in-Publication Data
is available

ISBN: 0-00-765375-1

10 9 8 7 6 5 4 3 2 1

Typeset in Sabon and Syntax
Color reproduction by Scanhouse
Printed and bound in Singapore by Imago

DEDICATION

For Carole (1948–2001):

"May you go forth by day,

may you join with the sun disc,

and may his rays illuminate your face."

NOTES
The abbreviations CE and BCE are used throughout
this book:
CE Common Era (the equivalent of AD)
BCE Before the Common Era (the equivalent of BC)

Page 1: Painted coffin of a 21st-dynasty priest from
Thebes, which features a huge floral collar and red
straps crossed over his chest to form the outline of a
protective *sa* amulet.

Page 2: The final scene in the *Book of Caverns*, which
portrays the nocturnal journey of the sun, represented
by the central, ram-headed figure whose wings span
the width of the burial chamber of the female
pharaoh Tawosret (reigned ca. 1188–1186BCE), from
her tomb (KV.14) in the Valley of the Kings.

CONTENTS

INTRODUCTION

At the heart of ancient Egypt's civilization lay its highly complex religion, which evolved, expanded and diversified over more than 3,000 years. Understanding the essence of this religion is the key to a vast and at times bewildering legacy of myth and ritual, through which the wisdom of ancient Egypt reveals itself.

The central characters in the religion of the Egyptians were their gods and goddesses, whose numbers steadily increased over the millennia as both local and foreign gods were adopted into an all-embracing national belief system. So tolerant was this system that it was able to accommodate a wide range of apparently contradictory myths and legends. However, these often conflicting accounts were regarded as essentially complementary, and the priesthood that skilfully wove them together was reluctant to discard anything of divinely-inspired origin. In this way the Egyptians were able to accept many variations on important religious themes – hence there were several accounts of the creation of the world, all regarded as equally valid.

The flexibility of the resulting religious framework was the secret of its extraordinary durability – it simply absorbed and adapted new elements in an open-minded way. The hold of the old beliefs only loosened in the early centuries CE, following the loss of national independence to Rome. This bleak period for the native Egyptians coincided with the rise of Christianity, whose converts coexisted with the practitioners of the old religion until, in the fourth century CE, the Romans declared Christianity to be the sole permitted faith of the empire and ordered the closure of all non-Christian places of worship. By 400CE the ancient religion was virtually dead and with it died the culture of ancient Egypt.

In many ways the religion of the Egyptians was based on the concept of dualities, whereby everything in the universe was balanced by its opposite in a state of perfect equilibrium (*maat*). This idea originated in the stark contrasts of their own environment, with Kemet (the "Black Land"), the fertile banks of the life-giving river Nile on which they lived, set against Deshret (the "Red Land"), the vast and barren deserts. In this way, day was balanced by night and life was balanced by death – which meant a continuation of life in a parallel world, envisioned as an idealized form of Egypt. The location of the afterlife could be placed in the heavens, although it was generally described as an underworld. Here the dead lived eternally as blessed transfigured spirits, or *akh*s, once they had undertaken the perilous journey through the darkness of the underworld and successfully faced the judgment of the god Osiris.

Most fundamentally for the Egyptian world-view, order was balanced by chaos. The Egyptians did all in their power to regulate and control this cosmic equilibrium, which they believed could be maintained only with the co-operation of their numerous gods and goddesses. In a reciprocal arrangement, the deities kept the universe in order while their vital role was acknowledged by daily acts of worship and a constant flow of offerings which replenished their powers.

The gods and goddesses held back the forces of chaos through their earthly representative, the pharaoh (king). The image of the king as the intermediary between the mortal and divine worlds, interceding with the gods and goddesses for Egypt's benefit, adorned almost every available surface of every temple in the land.

The Egyptians recorded their beliefs in a wide range of media, from tomb and temple walls to wooden coffins and papyrus rolls. Accounts of these beliefs were later recorded by Greek and Roman scholars who were fascinated by a civilization that was already ancient in their day and keen to make sense of its complex religion. Through a combination of these Classical accounts, together with the countless discoveries made by Egyptologists over the years since the decipherment of the hieroglyphs early in the 19th century, it is possible today to piece together the Egyptians' unique view of life, death and the cosmos, upon which they built a culture that endured for more than three millennia.

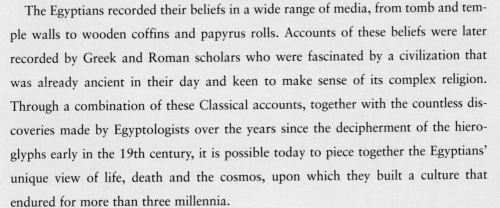

ORDER
OUT OF
CHAOS

Egypt's all-embracing framework of myths encompassed at least three accounts of creation. They were all interconnected, but each centred on a particular creator deity or group of deities: the Nine Gods of Heliopolis, the Eight Gods of Hermopolis and Ptah, the god of Memphis, Egypt's traditional capital. All were credited with creating the universe and their priests all claimed that their temple stood on the very site where creation had begun.

THE SELF-CREATED LORD

The earliest of Egypt's creation myths claims that the supreme creator was Atum, whose name means "the all" or "the complete". A solar deity, Atum was simply an aspect of the great sun god Ra (see page 44), and their two names were often combined to form the composite deity Ra-Atum or Atum-Ra. His powers were so great that he was considered to be self-created, and is described as "the great god who took form of himself" and "creator uncreated". Atum was the Lord of Iunu in Lower Egypt, better known by its Greek name of Heliopolis, "City of the Sun". The myth is first mentioned in the *Pyramid Texts*, funerary inscriptions on the inner walls of some Old Kingdom royal pyramids.

In the beginning, Atum emerged silently from Nun, the dark waters of chaos, on top of the primeval hill (see box opposite). "The one who came into being of himself" contained the universal life force, and so Atum was able to create life entirely alone, although the *Pyramid Texts* give two versions of how this miraculous act was achieved. In the first version, Atum "takes his phallus in his fist and ejaculates to give birth to the twin gods Shu and Tefnut", the deities of air and moisture. Alternatively, he simply "sneezed out Shu and spat out Tefnut". Thus "he who was one became three". The force of their unusual birth flung Shu and Tefnut out into the waters of Nun.

The god Atum is shown enthroned wearing the royal double crown of Egypt in this wall painting from the tomb of Nefertari, queen of Ramses II (ruled ca. 1279–1213BCE), Western Thebes. In his right hand he holds an *ankh*, or "key of life", indicating his life-giving role as the creator sun god.

When Atum found them again he embraced them "so that his *ka* [soul] might be in them". Once infused with the creator's force, they in turn were able to have intercourse in the normal human way and produce their own children.

Tefnut initiated the next stage of creation by giving birth to the earth god Geb and the sky goddess Nut. Atum placed Shu between Geb and Nut to create the basic structure of the universe. Beyond Nut's arched body, which formed the sky, Atum had pushed back the Nun to encircle the universe and, as "Lord of the Limits of the Sky", it was he who prevented the waters of chaos from crashing through the sky to engulf and destroy the world.

This ancient solar legend was adapted by the priesthood of Heliopolis to incorporate the myth of the god Osiris and emphasize his descent from the sun god. Before

THE PRIMEVAL HILL

The site of creation was imagined as a mound of earth, the primeval hill, on which the sun was born. The hill rose out of the formless waters of Nun, reflecting the way in which the land re-emerged from the receding waters of the annual Nile flood. The shape of the Great Pyramid (right) and later pyramids is believed to represent the primeval hill. A gilded capstone, or pyramidion, was originally set at the apex of each pyramid to catch the first rays of the dawn sun and transmit its reviving powers down into the king's burial chamber. The hill was also replicated as the *benben*, a pyramid-shaped stone venerated in the temple of the sun at Heliopolis.

Geb and Nut were separated, they had intercourse to produce four children of their own: Osiris, Isis, Nephthys and Seth. Their presence makes the Heliopolitan creation myth a story of nine gods, collectively known as the Ennead, from the Greek for "nine". It was their inter-family feuding that first brought death into the world (see pages 60–63).

Following the creation of the great Ennead, Egypt's many other gods came into being along with everything else in the universe. The creation of human beings was something of an afterthought. Humankind came into being when the sun god wept. As his tears fell to earth, they became people, a transformation which relies on a play on the ancient Egyptian words for "tears" (*remyt*) and "people" (*remet*). However, almost as soon as they were created, humans brought themselves to the edge of destruction in a story first inscribed on the shrines in the tomb of Tutankhamun.

THE EYE OF RA

The female deity known as the "Eye of Ra" often takes the form of the benign and beautiful goddess Hathor, who is commonly represented as a cow and is most familiar in her role as a nurturing mother-figure. But Hathor was only one aspect of a deity who was able to transform herself instantly into a terrifying force of vengeance and destruction. In this other guise she took the form of the ferocious lioness goddess Sekhmet ("Powerful One"), and it was in this guise that the sun god unleashed his daughter upon humankind.

Hathor-Sekhmet was also known as the "Lady of Drunkenness" – a reference to the way in which the sun god tricked his daughter into ending her slaughter of humankind (see main text, opposite) – and the Egyptians would drink great quantities of beer in her honour.

The sun god ruled over the world he had created, an elderly deity with bones of silver, flesh of gold and hair of lapis lazuli. During an idyllic golden age, the earth flourished beneath his benign rays, yet despite all the benefits he brought them, humans began to undermine his authority and plotted against him. Furious at this betrayal, the sun god decided to retaliate and punish the ungrateful human race. He summoned a meeting of all the deities in his solar palace to tell them of his intentions. They all consented to his plan and unanimously agreed that the agent of destruction should be the "Eye of Ra" – the sun god's own daughter and the most fearsome of deities (see box opposite).

Although the treacherous humans tried to run for their lives and hide in the desert, the fierce lioness deity hunted them down and revelled in their slaughter as she waded through their blood. As one papyrus puts it: "The Eye of Ra appears against you, she devours you, she punishes you."

However, the terrible suffering he had inflicted moved the sun god to end the slaughter before the human race was completely annihilated. During the night, while the Eye slept soundly, Ra ordered his aides to "run as swift as the shadows" to the region of Aswan in southern Egypt and gather great quantities of red ochre. The ochre was taken to the high priest of the sun god at Heliopolis with instructions to add it to seven thousand jars of strong beer. Just before dawn, this potent red liquid was poured over the land to a height of "three palms".

The goddess awoke to see what she believed to be a vast lake of human blood, and immediately began to gulp it down. She soon became so drunk that she forgot her plan to destroy humankind and returned to her father's palace to sleep off the effects of the alcohol. In this way humans were spared their fate.

Yet the sun god was still deeply saddened by human deceit. Exhausted by the thankless task of governing the earth, Ra decided to withdraw into the heavens, with the help of his son Shu and granddaughter Nut, the air and the sky. But humans would not be completely abandoned when the sun god left them, and Ra appointed the wise god Thoth, "scribe of the Ennead", as their guardian and teacher.

THE ISLAND OF FIRE

The second creation story originated in Khemnu ("Eight Town"), the cult centre of the god Thoth and better known as Hermopolis, "City of Hermes", since the Greeks equated Thoth with Hermes. Khemnu's name links it with eight deities known as the Ogdoad, from the Greek for "eight", who were described as "the fathers and mothers who were before the original gods" and "the ancestors of the sun".

The Hermopolitan myth also begins with the dark primeval waters. Latent within the womb-like waters were the basic forces from which life could be created, personified as the Ogdoad: the male gods Nun, Heh, Kek and Amun; and their female equivalents

This scene from *The Book of the Dead* of Khonsumose, a priest of the 21st Dynasty (ca. 1075–945 BCE), shows the Ogdoad as simple figures wielding hoes to create the primeval mound. They could also appear as plain discs to suggest their mysterious, abstract quality, or as frogs (Nun, Heh, Kek and Amun) and snakes (Naunet, Hauhet, Kauket and Amunet) – the first creatures seen as the annual Nile flood receded.

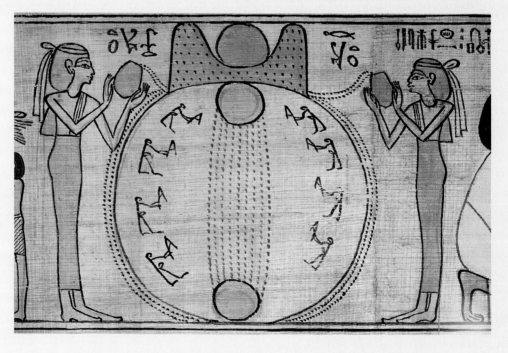

Naunet, Hauhet, Kauket and Amunet. Nun and Naunet represented the forces of the primeval waters; Heh and Hauhet infinity (or the force of the flood); Kek and Kauket darkness; and Amun (see box below) and Amunet the hidden life force. The energy of their couplings unleashed such powerful combustion across the primeval waters it brought into being the primeval mound, here called the "Isle of Flame". Following this first act of creation, the sun burst forth from the fiery mound in the very first dawn.

In declaring that the Ogdoad had created the sun, the priests of Hermopolis claimed that their theology was more ancient than that of Heliopolis. The temple of Hermopolis even housed supposed fragments of the "cosmic egg" from which the sun god had hatched. This refers to a later adaptation of the myth in which Thoth positioned the egg on top of the Isle of Flame as a place whence the sun could be born.

AMUN THE CREATOR

As the Hermopolis myth continued to evolve, the individual deities of the Ogdoad began to develop independently. This was especially true of Amun (right), who embodied the masculine creative principle. Evolving through a complex pattern of myths from a divine frog into a divine king, his career took him from a relatively minor role as one of eight creator gods to become Egypt's supreme deity (see pages 52–57). This development was centred on Amun's great cult at Karnak.

Eventually Amun came to be considered the sole creator of the universe. Like Atum (see page 10), he contained both male and female within himself and brought himself into being before anything else existed. Through a mysterious process only hinted at, his "fluid and form" combined to produce the cosmic egg of creation. An account from the Ptolemaic Period calls Amun "father of the semen, mother of the egg, who created everything that lives, hidden soul who made the gods."

PTAH THE CRAFTSMAN

The third major creation myth centred on the ancient Egyptian capital of Memphis (Ineb-hedj or Mennefer) and its most important deity, Ptah. Memphis was once the site of an enormous temple called Huwt-ka-Ptah – the "Mansion of the Soul of Ptah" – that may be the origin of the Greek word "Aigyptos", from which the name "Egypt" derives. Worshipped from the beginning of Egyptian history, Ptah's central role in creation was first set down at least as early as the Middle Kingdom. However, the main surviving source is a copy in stone made on the orders of King Shabaka (ruled ca. 716–702BCE) when the original ancient papyrus scroll in the temple of Ptah was discovered to be damaged. The inscription refers to the king by his standard title of "son of Ra" (*sa Ra*) but he is also called the son of Ptah: "His Majesty found this work of the ancestors to be worm-eaten and … copied it anew so that it was better than before, in order that it may endure forever, as a work done by the son of Ra for his father Ptah." (Unfortunately for Egyptologists, when the "Shabaka Stone" was rediscovered in the early 20th century a farmer was using it to grind flour. The stone had been pierced through the middle and parts of the inscription were lost.)

According to the priests of Ptah, their god was responsible for the whole of creation. To stress his pre-eminence, he was combined with both the masculine and feminine aspects of the waters of chaos as Ptah-Nun and Ptah-Naunet, and was referred to as "the father who bore Atum, the

This gilded statuette of Ptah was found in the tomb of Tutankhamun (ruled ca. 1332–1322BCE) and depicts him with close-cropped hair in the manner of an artisan. His staff combines the *djed* pillar (meaning stability), *was* sceptre (dominion) and *ankh* sign (life).

mother who bore Atum". In *The Memphite Theology*, a remarkably sophisticated creation account developed by the priests at Memphis, the universe is formed simply through the power of Ptah's "heart" (that is, his mind or intellect, which the Egyptians believed to be located in the heart). After thinking the world and all living things – including the gods – into being, he then made them a reality through the simple process of uttering their names – a concept not unlike the Judeo-Christian idea of the creative Word of God:

"The gods came into being through Ptah, Atum took shape in his heart and on his tongue. For the very greatest is Ptah, who gave life to all the gods and their *ka*s [souls] through his heart and his tongue, in which Horus has taken shape as Ptah, in which

THE CREATOR GODDESS: NEITH

In contrast to the three major creation myths which feature male or androgynous gods, the goddess Neith was also credited with being the primordial creator deity, emerging from the waters of Nun at the beginning of time. Texts at Esna temple claim that Neith emerged there as creator before being carried by the Nile to her main temple at Sais in the Delta.

She was said to have called the universe into being by uttering seven statements that were later regarded as her thunderous, sevenfold peals of laughter. Like Ptah, she moulded the first humans. A stela refers to King Amenhotep II (ruled ca. 1426–1401BCE), "whose being Neith fashioned", and other kings were hailed as "son of Neith". In her maternal guise she was both "Neith the Great, Mother of Ra" and the "Great Radiant One", mother of the crocodile god Sobek and even of the evil serpent Apophis. But like many of Egypt's mother goddesses, she also possessed a destructive aspect. She was closely associated with war and her powers were said to be so great that she could threaten to make the sky collapse and destroy the world she had created.

Thoth has taken shape as Ptah. Ptah is in the mouth of all the gods, all humans, all cattle, all creeping things that live. The Ennead of Ptah are his teeth and lips, they are the semen and the hands of Atum. All the gods were born and his Ennead was complete. For every word of the god came about through that which his heart thought of and his tongue summoned forth. And Ptah is Tatenen [the primeval hill], who gave birth to the gods, and from whom all things came forth. He is the mightiest of all the gods, satisfied at what he has made."

After creating all things, Ptah perfected them through his skills as an artisan. Like the ram-headed god Khnum (see pages 20–21), Ptah was a craftsman – the high priest of Ptah at Memphis bore the title "Greatest of the Controllers of the Craftsmen". Unsurprisingly, Ptah was a very popular deity among working people, especially skilled artisans, who regarded him as their patron deity. For them Ptah was *mesedjer sedjem* – "the ear that hears" – and to him they addressed their prayers. In a 13th-Dynasty worker's prayer to the god, a washerman called Hepet says: "Hail O Ptah, Lord of Life of the Two Lands, I am here before you to worship you, as a servant who does not forget his duties at your festivals." One of Ptah's epithets is *nefer-her*, meaning "beautiful of face", yet the god is generally portrayed as a rather static-looking, androgynous figure wearing a close-fitting robe and an artisan's skullcap, with his hands tightly clasping his sceptre in front of him.

Also referred to as "Lord of Truth" (*maat*), Ptah was believed to administer "justice to those who do what is loved and punishment to those who do what is hated … life for the peaceful and death for the criminal". On a small stone stela, a workman called Neferabu from Deir el-Medina, the tomb builders' village near the Valley of the Kings, admits that he had sworn "a false oath on the name of Ptah, Lord of Truth", and as a consequence had been blinded by the god. He warns: "Beware of the Lord of Truth, who sees everyone's deeds!"

In death, it was Ptah – represented by the *sem* priest (see pages 93–94) – who performed the vital "Opening of the Mouth" ceremony for the deceased, which begins with the words: "My mouth is opened by Ptah." (See page 118.)

MAAT, THE DIVINE ORDER

The universe was created in a state of perfect balance and it was necessary to maintain it at all costs. Following the creation of the world, the goddess Maat came into being as the personification of universal order and the embodiment of the concept of truth. She was the means by which all should live, even the gods themselves. The creator god Atum is instructed in one text to "inhale your daughter Maat … so that your heart can live", while in another, Amun-Ra, the king of the gods, is told that "Maat is breath for your nose, your bread is Maat and your beer is Maat".

The guidance of Maat had to be followed by all to prevent the forces of chaos from undermining the cosmic order, which she represented. In the afterlife, where the blessed dead were said to "live in Maat", she continued to maintain justice, standing beside the throne of Osiris, "Lord of Maat", in order to guide him as he judged the dead (see pages 124–125).

Depicted as the daughter of Ra and as the sister of the king, Maat is generally represented as a woman with a tall feather on her head. This figure also represents her name in hieroglyphs, but it could also be written either as a feather alone or as a symbol that probably represents the primeval mound – indicating Maat's vital role in maintaining creation since the very beginning of time.

THE CREATION OF HUMANKIND

In Egyptian mythology the creation of human beings occurs as something of an after-thought to the main process of establishing the universe and the gods' place in it. Per-haps the most striking account describes how humans were created of clay on a potter's wheel by the ram-headed creator god Khnum (opposite), who was wor-shipped on the island of Elephantine at Aswan and at Esna. *The Great Hymn to Khnum*, chanted each year at the god's festival at Esna, hails Khnum as the creator of all life and gives the following account of how he made humans:

"He knotted veins to the bones
　Made in his workshop as his own
　　creation:
So the breath of life is in all things.
The bones fastened together from
　the start.

He made hair grow,
Fastened skin to the limbs,
He built the skull and formed the face,
To give shape to the image.

He opened the eyes, carved out
　the ears,
He made the body inhale,
He hollowed out the mouth for eating
And the throat for swallowing,
The tongue to speak, the jaws to open,
　the throat to drink, swallow and spit.

He made the spine for support,
The hands and fingers to do their work,
The heart to guide,
The penis to beget and the womb
　to conceive
And increase the people in Egypt;

The feet to step and legs to tread,
The bones performing their task
By the desire of his heart.

Forming all humans on his wheel,
Their speech different in each country
　and to that of Egypt –
For the Lord of the Wheel is their
　father, too –
And making all that is in their lands,
As his mouth spat out they were born
As his wheel turns every day without pause."

THE COSMIC BUBBLE

The Egyptians personified the elements and more abstract concepts as gods and goddesses, whose complex interaction maintained the structure of a cosmos that was generally believed to constitute three basic parts: Sky, Earth and Underworld. The sky was often regarded as an endless sea, within which the earth existed as a kind of "bubble". Egypt's predominantly water-based cosmology reflected the country's dependence on the Nile as its source of life.

CHILDREN OF THE SUN

According to the creation myth of Heliopolis, in which the sun god created the universe (see pages 10–13), he also produced the gods as his children. His first-born were Shu and Tefnut, the twin deities of air and moisture. These abstract concepts were personified in a number of ways. Representing the notion of air filled with sunlight, Shu is often depicted in human form as a kneeling man with a feather on his head. The feather, which is also an element in his written name, relates to the air and is suggestive of weightlessness. The name "Shu" is regarded as onomatopoeic, since in one account of his birth the sun god brought him into being with a giant sneeze.

As the embodiment of the atmosphere, Shu has a range of crucial functions. According to the *Pyramid Texts*, Shu and the sun god assist the king to ascend to the heavens: "The hand of the king in the hand of Ra, O Shu, lift him up!" During the Amarna Period, the god is described as "Shu-who-is-in-Aten", one with the sun itself, while in a later inscription of the pharaoh Merneptah (ruled ca. 1213–1203BCE), it is Shu who makes it possible for sunlight to reach the earth since he is the one who disperses the clouds and lets "Egypt see the sun's rays". In funerary texts Shu's powers are invoked on behalf of the deceased, as in this inscription on a sarcophagus lid of a man called Wennofer: "May Shu send you the sweet north wind, the breath of life to your nose."

Shu can also be portrayed as a lion, like his partner Tefnut. Personifying moisture, Tefnut is said to have been spat out by the sun god, and her name can sometimes be written with a hieroglyph of spitting lips. The same imagery occurs in *The Memphite Theology* on the Shabaka Stone (see page 16), which speaks of the "teeth and lips" of the creator god Ptah, "which spoke the name of every thing, from which Shu and Tefnut came forth". As a daughter of the sun god, Tefnut is one manifestation of the fierce "Eye of Ra" (see page 12).

Infused with the powers of the creator, Shu and Tefnut in turn produced their own children, the twins Geb (the earth) and Nut (the sky), to initiate the next stage of creation and give structure to the universe. Unlike many ancient peoples, the Egyptians imagined the earth as masculine, with the male god Geb regarded as "the eldest [son] of Shu" and appearing in the *Pyramid Texts* and in *The Memphite Theology* as "Lord of the Gods", presiding over their quarrels as judge in the Hall of Geb, as during the long feud between Horus and Seth (see pages 64–67). Geb also appears as the father of the king, whose seat is referred to as "the throne of Geb". At death, the king is greeted by Geb: "Rejoicing at your coming, [Geb] gives you his hands and kisses you, setting you among the Imperishable Stars", and in a passage from the *Coffin Texts*, the deceased declares: "I have spent a million years dwelling with Geb in one place."

When Nut and Geb were created, Geb lay beneath Nut and she conceived their four children: Isis, Osiris, Seth and Nephthys. But this left no space between the earth and

GEB, THE GOD OF EARTH

Geb is generally pictured as a reclining man, sometimes coloured green to symbolize the fecundity of the land and the crops which sprout from his body. He can also be represented by a goose, which is the hieroglyph for his name. In one account of creation, the cackling of this primordial bird, known as the "Great Honker" (*gengen wer*), was the first sound and it caused the cosmic egg to crack open and release all life. The power of Geb's resounding utterances is also reflected in the idea that earthquakes were his laughter, while thunder was the laughter of his sister, the sky goddess Nut.

The goddess Nut emerges from a sycamore tree with offerings of water and a tray of loaves for the deceased (right), a priest named Khonsumose, indicating that he will never want for sustenance in the afterlife. A vignette from *The Book of the Dead* of Khonsumose, 21st Dynasty (ca. 1075–945BCE).

sky for life to exist, so Atum placed their father Shu, the air, between them. In his capacity as god of air, Shu embodied the atmosphere in which life could exist, and forever after his ethereal form held apart the supine green body of his son Geb and the star-spangled torso of his daughter Nut (see box, page 25). Her heavenly realm was regarded as the home of the gods, and the *Pyramid Texts* refer to the time when "the sky was split from the earth and the gods went into the sky".

A goddess of incalculable power, whose epithets include "Mysterious One", Nut literally upheld the order of the universe. With her hands and feet at the four cardinal points, her great arched body held back the waters of chaos, which had been pushed out to encircle the created world. The Egyptians believed that if they failed to maintain order on earth, then chaos would triumph as its waters crashed through the sky to engulf and destroy the world. Nut is described in this prayer of the king from the *Pyramid Texts*: "Great One who became the sky, you are mighty, you are strong, filling all places with your beauty. The earth beneath you is in your possession and you enfold it in your arms."

The Egyptians believed that Nut gave birth to the sun each morning, the red of the early morning sky being the blood of childbirth. The sun god then travelled along the underside of her body by day before she swallowed him at every sunset. Nut's name is often translated as "the Watery One", reflecting the idea that the sun god sailed across the waters of Nut by day before disappearing each evening. After being swallowed by Nut the sun god either passed through her body or sailed through the dark region called Duat until dawn (see pages 44–49). Although it is usually referred to as the "underworld", the Egyptians in fact more often placed Duat in the sky than below the earth, and Duat is sometimes described as lying within the body of Nut to unify the various versions of their cosmology.

The goddess's important role in Egyptian solar mythology is seen in her title "Lady of Heliopolis" – the centre of sun worship – although Nut herself had no temple. However, in keeping with the way in which Egyptian deities frequently share their roles and attributes, Nut shares her maternal role in the mythology of the sun with other goddesses who are described as the "Mother of Ra" to enhance their status. For example, Neith is hailed on one statue as "Neith the Great, the mother of god, the mother who bore Ra before birth had yet been".

Nut's role in the rebirth of the sun each day was paralleled by her similarly vital function in the resurrection of the dead, for whom she acted in a maternal, protective capacity. In the *Pyramid Texts*, the dead king's afterlife journey is equated with the passage of the sun god, and the *Pyramid Texts* refer to the moment at which the king "is just before heaven and earth, just before this earth to which he has swum, to which he has come and which lies between the thighs of Nut". Elsewhere in the *Pyramid Texts*, Nut leads the deceased king by the hand and he joins her in the heavens in the

form of a star. These writings also speak of Nut enfolding the king – her son, since he was identified with Osiris – in her arms, "concealing you from evil, protecting you from evil" – an idea graphically conveyed by the image of the dark blue sky and golden stars painted on the ceilings of royal burial chambers.

As "Mistress of All", Nut was portrayed in the form of a woman on the inside of coffin lids, an image that expresses the wish of the deceased that, as the Middle King-dom *Story of Sinuhe* puts it, the goddess may "spend eternity above me", stretched out over the body to protect and sustain it forever. The same idea is expressed in the figure of Nut that appears as part of the protective bead net that was sometimes draped over the chest of the wrapped mummy. Again in a sustaining role, Nut can be depicted emerging from the sacred sycamore tree to provide air and water for the deceased in the afterlife.

Generally portrayed as a svelte woman of slender proportions, whether arching over the earth or emerging from the sycamore, Nut can also appear as the celestial cow or even as a sow nursing piglets, an image intended to convey her fertile nurtur-ing qualities. Even more rarely, Nut can take the form of a bee.

On the inside of this coffin lid of the 2nd century CE, the sky goddess Nut extends her protective embrace over the deceased, a man called Soter. Nut is surrounded by zodiac animals and figures representing the hours of the day. Between her feet the sun, depicted as a scarab, is reborn at dawn.

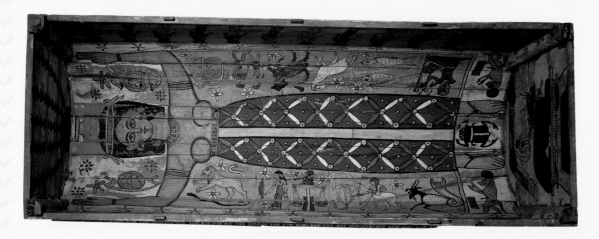

TATENEN AND AKER

Within the Egyptian tripartite cosmic structure of Sky, Earth and Duat were other gods who shared Geb's role as an earth deity. One of these, Tatenen, was an aspect of Ptah and represented the primeval mound of earth that rose from the waters of chaos (see page 11), while Aker was an ancient god associated with both the earth and Duat. The solar role of Geb, Tatenen and Aker is found in the extensive inscriptions on the walls of the burial chamber of Ramses VI (ruled ca. 1145–1137BCE), which are known collectively as *The Book of the Earth*.

Depicted as a section of land with a human head, Aker could also be portrayed either as a double-headed figure with human or lion heads, or as a pair of lions seated back to back facing opposite directions, an image referred to as the "lions of yesterday and tomorrow". The idea of looking both ways accompanied Aker's role as guardian of the gateways to the underworld, which were located at the western and eastern horizons and marked by the mountains known to the Egyptians as Manu and Bakhu. Having entered the underworld through the western gateway each evening, the sun god could then travel along Aker's back during the night in much the same way as he could also be said to travel through the body of the sky goddess Nut.

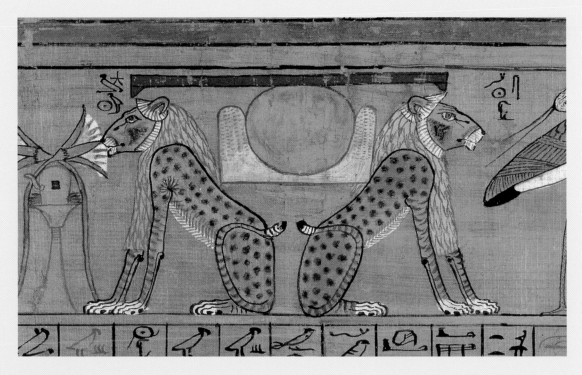

THE RIVER OF LIFE

The Greek historian Herodotus, who travelled in Egypt in the fifth century BCE, said that "Egypt is the gift of the Nile", a statement that exactly expresses the relationship between the country and its river. Without the Nile, there would be no Egypt – a fact the Egyptians fully appreciated, for only they had such a great and permanent source of water, while neighbouring lands had to rely on erratic rainfall.

The rhythms of the Nile, which the Egyptians called simply "the river" (*iteru*), dictated the pace of life as its waters rose and fell during the course of the year and its annual cycle of flooding and drought fixed the Egyptian calendar. There were three

A HYMN TO HAPI

The annual arrival of Hapi, the god of the inundation, was an occasion of great rejoicing. This is expressed in the hymn sung to Hapi at this time, composed in the Middle Kingdom but surviving in later copies. This is an extract:

"Hail to you, Hapi,
Sprung from the earth and come to feed Egypt!
You flood the fields created by Ra,
Refreshing all who are thirsty. …
Every belly rejoices,
Every mouth laughs
And teeth are revealed in smiles!
Conqueror of the Two Lands,
You fill the storehouses,
You make the barns bulge
And give bounty to the poor."

A fragment of wall painting from the tomb of the 18th-Dynasty scribe Nebamun shows him hunting birds on the Nile, accompanied on his papyrus punt by his wife and daughter. The scene is both a depiction of a popular pastime of the wealthy and a metaphor for the imposition of order on the chaos of the natural world, represented by the startled birds. Reign of Amenhotep III, ca. 1390–1353BCE.

seasons: *akhet* (inundation), *peret* (planting) and *shemu* (harvest). The Egyptian New Year's Day (19th July) marked the start of the inundation, heralded by the appearance of Sirius, the brightest star in the night sky (see box, page 41).

Although the Nile was generally regarded as a benign force, if its annual flood-waters (actually caused by the heavy summer rains in the highlands of Ethiopia) did not rise sufficiently then famine would occur (see box, page 33). Yet if the waters rose too high there would also be disaster, because the mudbrick homes in which most people lived would be washed away. It was therefore essential that the gods were on hand to regulate the river's flow. The ram-headed creator god Khnum (see page 21) was generally credited with causing the Nile to emerge from its source – which was believed to be in the underworld – at his temple on Elephantine Island, close to Egypt's southern frontier. Khnum, "who drenches the land with the waters of Nun", directed the waters from his cave at the rocky cataracts near modern Aswan.

As the god of resurrection and fertility, Osiris also played an important role in the annual cycle of the Nile. As the ruler of the underworld it was he who ordained that

the inundation should begin each year. As the waters rose to revive the land, they were seen to act in the same way as Osiris, who restored the dead to life.

The life-giving powers of the waters were personified by the god Hapi, a plump androgynous figure who brought fertility and abundance to the land through the annual flood, which was described as either a "large Hapi" or a "small Hapi" depending on the height of the waters. Pairs of Hapi figures are often portrayed tying together the heraldic plants of the lotus (Upper Egypt) and the papyrus (Lower Egypt), symbolizing the way in which the Nile both united the land and brought it wealth. The king is also sometimes portrayed as Hapi to show his ability to bring blessings and abundance to his people. Certain statues of the pharaoh Amenhotep III (ruled ca. 1390–1352BCE) depict him in this way. The floodwaters themselves were embodied by the cow goddess Mehetweret, "the Great Flood", who represented the female nurturing aspect of the waters and was associated with Nut and Hathor.

The creatures that dwelt in the river all had a place in the Nile's rich mythology. Crocodiles and hippopotami were both feared and revered as powerful gods in their own right. The crocodile god Sobek was honoured at Kom Ombo and in the Fayuum oasis, where crocodile attacks were particularly common. The ferocity of Taweret, the hippopotamus goddess, was invoked during childbirth to drive away evil (see pages 72–73). The waterfowl of the Nile had a wide variety of roles, with many species embodying aspects of major gods. The goose was associated with Amun and Geb, the ibis was the sacred bird of Thoth, and herons were associated with the rebirth of the sun. The fish which filled the river also had divine connections, with tilapia fish regarded as emblems of Hathor and symbols of resurrection, because their habit of swallowing their young in times of danger and later spitting them out again was seen as an act of self-generation. Even the common frog had a place in the divine scheme, with the four male creator deities of the Ogdoad perceived as frogs, while the frog goddess Heket was a deity involved in the creative act of childbirth.

Both fish and fowl were seen as part of the Nile's bounty sent to the people by the gods, and scenes of fishing and hunting on the river are frequent in funerary art. On one level they represent the way in which the abundance of the river sustains life both in this world and the next. On another, they show the tomb owner actively bringing order to the chaos of the natural world, which is hinted at by the flapping of startled birds and the menacing crocodiles lurking beneath the water. The deceased takes on a role similar to that of the sun god, who sails across the heavens by day and through the underworld by night, defeating the forces of chaos.

The Nile was also Egypt's most important highway. Unlike, for example, the Euphrates – which the Egyptians called "Reversed Water" – the Nile flows south to north. Northward journeys took advantage of the current, but southerly travel had to rely on the wind. This is reflected in the hieroglyphs for "travelling north", which shows a boat without sails, while "travelling south" has a boat with sails unfurled.

A TIME OF FAMINE

Carved directly into the rock of Sehel Island at Aswan is the "Famine Stela" (right), an inscription that dates to Ptolemaic times but refers to events which it claims had occurred more than 2,000 years earlier, in the reign of King Djoser (ruled ca. 2667–2648BCE). The stela records how Djoser beseeched the god Khnum to restore the Nile inundations, which had been disastrously low for seven years. One passage vividly evokes the sufferings of the people when the inundation failed: "Grain was scarce, food was hard to find, and neighbour stole from neighbour. Children cried and the old were in grief, their legs drawn up as they hugged the ground, clasping their arms about them. All were in distress."

A WORLD OF DUALITIES

Ancient Egyptian religion was founded upon the concept of dualities, or pairs. For the Egyptians, the most important duality was that of order and chaos, a notion rooted in the Egyptian landscape of fertile, habitable river margins hemmed in by vast, wild and inhospitable desert. In myth, this duality was expressed most fundamentally in the emergence of life from the cosmic waters of Nun, the eternal primordial "one", at the beginning of the world. The Egyptians described the time before creation as a "time before two things existed" (*Coffin Texts*); everything which sprang into being following the miraculous act of creation was countered and balanced by its opposite, without which it could not exist. Thus the universe was in a state of perfect equilibrium, or cosmic symmetry, which was both personified and maintained by the goddess Maat (see page 19).

Held back since the time of creation by the sky goddess Nut, the cosmic waters were the place from which life first arose, and it was from its depths that the world had emerged. This scenario was graphically echoed each year when the land re-emerged from the receding floodwaters of the Nile covered with new deposits of the rich dark alluvial silt that gave the country its ancient Egyptian name of Kemet, the "Black Land". Kemet was a place of order and civilization under the rule of the king, the god Horus incarnate, as opposed to Deshret, the "Red Land" of the desert, a barren and hostile place under the rule of the volatile and chaotic Seth. But every time they rejoiced to see the life-giving waters of the Nile rising to inundate and irrigate the land, the Egyptians were also keenly aware that if the river rose too high it also had the power to bring about cataclysmic destruction.

Everything else in the universe had its essential counterpart. Life and death were simply two aspects of the same state, the deceased passing into an afterlife which was regarded as a continuation of earthly life in all its aspects, but in a different realm: the underworld, or Duat, the landscape of which was identical to that of Egypt.

Life and death were mirrored by day and night, whose perfectly regular alternation was a constant reminder to the Egyptians of the way in which the gods controlled their universe. The lords of time were Ra, the sun god, and Osiris, the god of the underworld (Duat) and ruler of the dead. The sun god ruled the daytime and, according to the *Coffin Texts*, "created the night for the Weary-Hearted One [Osiris]".

The association of life with day and death with night was reflected in the imagery of the sun god, whose alternating journey through day and night reflected the journey of the individual through life and death. The sun was born each morning, aged through the day and sank each evening into the underworld of Osiris, disappearing into a darkness that was both night and the realm of death, to reappear at dawn. The sun's daily rebirth was regarded as confirmation that the dead too were constantly reborn to a blessed afterlife. In the profound depths of the underworld, the sun god and Osiris fused to become one deity, whose twofold aspects are explained in *The Book of the Dead*: "Osiris is yesterday and Ra is tomorrow" (see pages 45–49).

Egypt's gods were envisaged as living similar lives to those of

This fragment of limestone relief shows King Ramses II (ruled ca. 1279–1213BCE, left) receiving the breath of life from his divine father, Amun. The pharaoh wears the double crown, or *pschent*, a combination of the white crown of Upper Egypt and the red crown of Lower Egypt that symbolizes his rule over the "Two Lands" (see box, page 37).

Part of a list of Egypt's monarchs commissioned by Ramses II (ruled 1279–1213BCE) to adorn his own temple at Abydos. In the second and fourth columns from the left, reading downward, the cartouche (oval ring) containing the royal "throne name" is preceded by the hieroglyphs for "He of the Sedge and the Bee" (*nisu bity*), meaning "King of Upper and Lower Egypt". The sedge plant was a heraldic emblem of Upper Egypt and the bee of Lower Egypt.

humans, in a divine realm which paralleled the human one, but on a very different time scale – for example, one hour in the underworld was equivalent to one human life-span on earth. The intervention of the deities in the human world was essential to uphold *maat*, and this was based on a two-way arrangement: the gods would work to maintain the cosmic order for the benefit of humankind, who would reciprocate by sustaining their efforts with constant offerings. The intermediary between the human and divine worlds was the king, whose person was also marked by inherent dualities. The son of mortals, he (or indeed she) was also the son of the gods and their representative on earth. In this role – and some kings claimed to be solely of divine parentage – he was regarded as the incarnation of Horus, the son of Osiris, but he was also revered as the son of Amun,

Every deceased king was identified with Osiris, whose murder brought death into the world and so initiated the continuum of life and afterlife (see pages 58–61). It was also the first reminder to the world that where order reigned, chaos – in the shape of the turbulent god Seth – was rarely far away (see pages 64–67).

Egypt was often referred to as the "Two Lands", because the kingdom was divided both geographically and politically into Lower Egypt (the region of the Nile Delta) and Upper Egypt (from the base of the Delta to modern Aswan). One of the royal titles, the "throne name", is always prefaced by the phrase "King of Upper and Lower Egypt". In hieroglyphs this is written as "he of the sedge and the bee" (*nisu bity*), the sedge plant representing Upper Egypt and the bee Lower Egypt. The idea of the Two Lands united under the pharaoh's rule is also conveyed by the image of the intertwined lotus and papyrus, the heraldic plants of Upper and Lower Egypt respectively.

The Two Lands were represented in the royal regalia by the white crown of Upper Egypt and the red crown of Lower Egypt, which could be worn as individual crowns or in a combined form symbolizing the royal authority over a united kingdom. The crowns were associated with the two protective goddesses, Nekhbet the vulture (Upper Egypt) and Wadjyt the cobra (Lower Egypt), images of which the king wore on his brow to protect him from his enemies, as seen most spectacularly on the magnificent gold mask of Tutankhamun (see illustration).

Nekhbet's cult centre at Nekheb (el-Kab) in Upper Egypt was balanced by that of Wadjyt in the Lower Egyptian city of Buto (Tell el-Fara'in). This ancient "town twinning" is also seen in the way that certain towns of the same name existed in both Upper and Lower Egypt. Even Heliopolis, the great centre of the sun god in the north, was balanced by Thebes, "the Heliopolis of the South", where the sun god was worshipped as Amun-Ra. One of the two enormous seated statues of Amenhotep III known as the "Colossi of Memnon" bears an inscription that refers to the monuments being "brought from Heliopolis in Lower Egypt to Heliopolis in Upper Egypt" – a reference to the statues' origins in the stone quarries near the northern city and their final destination in the southern city.

WATERWAYS OF THE NIGHT

In the complex Egyptian view of the universe, the heavens were imagined as a great expanse of water, along which both gods and celestial bodies sailed by boat in a reflection of life on the Nile. The night sky was believed to be the location of the "Fields of Reeds", the ultimate destination of the deceased. Here, in an idealized version of Egypt, those who had successfully negotiated the perils of the underworld and judgment before Osiris (see pages 124–9) continued to live in a state of bliss, performing a minimum of work to yield an eternally bountiful crop.

To cross the heavenly waters required the services of a ferryman, called Mahaf in *The Book of the Dead* and referred to in the earlier *Pyramid Texts* as "Boatman of the Boatless Righteous, Ferryman in the Fields of Reeds". The *Pyramid Texts* locate the Fields of Reeds in the eastern sky, where the sun god was purified each morning together with the deceased king. The fields were also known as the "Fields of Offerings" and coffins were sometimes adorned for the benefit of the deceased with maps of this celestial region, complete with heavenly towns and geographical features such as "the Waterway of the White Hippopotamus", "the Waterway of the God [sic] Offering" and "the Sea of the Gods".

Elsewhere they are termed "Fields of the West" and are said to lie where the sun sets, at the gateway to the underworld. Yet another account locates the realm of the dead in the northern sky and associates the immortal deceased with the circumpolar stars, which never set – hence their Egyptian name of "the Imperishable Stars".

The ascent of the soul of the deceased into the heavens to become a star among the gods was initially a privilege restricted to the king alone. His stellar destination is referred to in the royal *Pyramid Texts*, where the sky goddess Nut invites the king to take his throne "among the stars of heaven". Thereafter the deceased king is regarded as "an indestructible spirit like the morning star above the flood". It is a motif found throughout royal funerary texts, with Seti I (ruled ca. 1294–1279BCE) described in a writing called *The Book of Night* as "Shining Bull who is with the Unwearying Stars".

As the afterlife became increasingly available to all, even non-royals could expect to be "enfolded in the embrace of Hathor, Lady of the Stars" in her capacity as the great "Celestial Cow" – Hathor's most ancient form, sharing the attributes of Nut, is a cow surrounded by stars (see pages 68–69). In one of the most beautiful passages of the *Pyramid Texts*, Nut is described as scattering the stars, whose green light was equated with the colour of vegetation and life: "Great Striding Goddess, sowing the green stones malachite and turquoise as stars, may the king be as green as are you, green as the living reed!" (Green turquoise was more highly prized than the pale blue variety.)

The Egyptians were keen astronomers and scanned the night sky from observatories on their temple roofs, using the movement of the stars to work out the passage of time and the seasons for both ritual and agricultural purposes. They divided the night sky into 36 decans, or groups of stars, each decan represented by a particular star god who travelled by boat across

The 12 familiar constellations of the zodiac are of Mesopotamian origin and were adopted by the ancient Egyptians only relatively late in their history, during the Ptolemaic Period. This artwork is based on the zodiac ceiling from Dendera (now at the Louvre), dedicated to a form of Hathor associated with the sky goddess Nut.

A fragment of New Kingdom wall painting depicting Osiris, who was identified with Orion. One of his numerous epithets was "he who dwells in Orion with a season in the sky and a season on earth".

the heavens for an annual period of ten days. This made up the Egyptian year of 360 days, to which five extra days were added to make up the full year (which however was still 0.25 days short). These five days were celebrated as the birthdays of Osiris, Isis, Horus, Seth and Nephthys.

The Egyptians identified the Milky Way, describing it evocatively as a "beaten pathway of stars" located "in the height of the sky". They also recognized numerous familiar constellations, including the Plough (Big Dipper) and Orion, which was represented by the god Sah, the consort of the goddess Sopdet or Sirius (see box opposite). Orion was also identified with Osiris and hence with the deceased king, who became one with Osiris when he rose up to the heavens at his death on the orders of Atum. There, he was transformed by Osiris's mother, the sky goddess Nut, into "an indestructible star". The process by which the king achieved this transformation is described in the *Pyramid Texts*: "Your hand is held by Ra, your head is raised by the Ennead. He comes as Orion, conceived of the sky, born of the Duat; you shall rise with Orion in the eastern sky and set with Orion in the western sky; Sirius is your guide on the sky paths, among the Fields of Reeds."

Images of the night sky decorate many temples and tombs, with "star clocks" of the decans inscribed on coffins and entire ceilings adorned with star-spangled images of Nut in blue and gold. During times of tumult, the Egyptians believed that the heavens teetered on the brink of chaos, when "the stars become dark, the heavens tremble, the earth shakes, and planets stand still". The ultimate cataclysm was envisaged as a time when "the stars are upturned and fall down on their faces, knowing not how to raise themselves again".

Egyptian astronomers identified five of the nine planets and called them "the stars who know no rest" (which means much the same as the Greek *planetes*, "wanderer"). They were believed to be deities who sailed through the sky. Three of the planets were identified with Horus, whose most ancient form was a sky god: "Horus who limits the Two Lands" (Jupiter); "Horus, Bull of the Sky" (Saturn); and "Red Horus" (Mars). Mercury was associated with the god Seth and Venus was a male deity, hailed as "God of the Morning" and also known as the "Lone Star". The planet was likened in the *Pyramid Texts* to the solitary splendour of the deceased king, "who looks down upon Osiris as he rules the spirit world, while you alone stand far from him".

SIRIUS

The Egyptians regarded Sirius, the Dog Star, as the most important star, because its appearance at dawn on around July 19th marked the New Year and heralded the onset of the annual Nile flood. The brightest star in the sky, Sirius was represented by the beautiful goddess Sopdet (Sothis in Greek), depicted as a woman with a star on her head and referred to as "Offspring of the Dawn" and "Bringer of the New Year and the Nile flood". One Egyptian poet describes his beloved as "the fairest of all, like the rising morning star at the start of a happy year". Sopdet was regarded as the sister of the deceased king and came to be associated with Isis.

Order out of Chaos

SAILING STARS

The Egyptians believed that the heavens were made of water and that the gods sailed across them. Initially they were envisaged – even the great Ra – as travelling on simple reed floats, everyday vessels used for hunting and fishing along the Nile and commonly depicted in tomb scenes. This image soon gave way to that of the celestial barque, a stately multi-oared vessel like those discovered near the Great Pyramid of Khufu and elsewhere, more befitting the gods' status and equipped with divine powers. The sun god travelled through the sky by day in his "day barque" before disappearing from view as he descended in the west and into the underworld, through which he travelled in his "night barque" (see page 45). In his wake the stars of the night propelled themselves through the nocturnal waters, praising the sun as they went, singing this hymn of praise to the sun from *The Book of the Dead*:

"Hail O Ra at your rising,
  You proceed at your pleasure in your night barque,
  Your heart is happy with a fair wind in the day barque,
  Filled with joy at crossing the sky with the blessed ones.

  All your enemies are crushed,
  The Unwearying Stars praise you,
  The Imperishable Stars worship you
  When you set on the horizon of Manu,
  Always happy and living forever as my lord."

THE REBIRTH OF THE SUN

Egypt was dominated by the sun. While the waters of the Nile brought life to their desert land, it was the sun which sustained this life and praise for the sun fills Egyptian literature: "Love for you fills the land when your rays fill all eyes, you are the well-being of all when you arise." As the sun rose each morning it caused the land to sparkle like a jewel. The sun was Egypt's pre-eminent deity and supreme creative force, and as such it penetrated all three realms of Sky, Earth and Duat.

Worshipped as both Ra and Atum at Egypt's main solar temple at Heliopolis, the sun god rose out of the primeval waters in order to create the universe, emerging as Atum upon the primeval mound in the first dawn (see pages 10–11). The sun was also said to have emerged as a newborn child from a lotus bud. This "golden youth" contained all the forces of light and heat, which burst forth to set creation in motion. For the Egyptians, the opening of the lotus's petals each dawn symbolized the release of the sun from the darkness of night. The sun god was also the "Great Cat", enemy of Apophis (Apep), the great serpent of chaos. Cats were kept to protect the home from evil, invoking the powers of "the tomcat who slew the serpent of chaos".

The classic Egyptian pyramid is believed to represent the mound on which the sun was born (see page 11). However, the very first pyramid, the Step Pyramid built at Sakkara by King Djoser of the Third Dynasty (left), is often thought to have been created as a stairway on which the king's immortal soul could ascend to the heavens. There he would take his place alongside the sun and the other gods.

The sun's daily journey was an eternal cycle of renewal symbolizing the triumph of life over death. By day the sun god crossed the sky in a great barque. At sunset he sank out of sight behind the western mountain of Manu to continue his voyage through the underworld for the 12 hours of the night. On this perilous journey the god had to combat the countless forces of chaos, led by Apophis, which did all they could to prevent him from reaching the eastern horizon of Bakhu. Aiding Ra in his battles were the forces of light and order, represented by Egypt's great deities and a host of other beings including Hu (Authority), Sia (Intellect) and Heka (Magic). They all sailed with the sun in his night barque on the waters of Duat, accompanied by the deceased king and, by the time of the Middle Kingdom, by the souls of all the blessed dead. During his nocturnal journey the sun god was referred to as "Flesh of Ra", represented with

THE BENU BIRD

The sun god is represented by a sacred bird called the *benu*, described in the *Coffin Texts* as "the form in which Atum came into being of himself". The bird is closely associated with the sun god's centre of Heliopolis, and there is a chapter in *The Book of the Dead* for transformation into a *benu* bird, so that the deceased might live again like the sun god. Initially portrayed as a yellow wagtail, the *benu* came to be depicted as a crested grey heron (right). The Greeks associated the *benu* with their mythical phoenix, and the *benu*'s connection with the sun and resurrection may have influenced the story of the phoenix dying in a pyre and rising from the ashes.

a ram's head as the "Sacred Ram of the West" and "Lord of the Underworld". The underworld was also the realm of Osiris, but the existence of two rulers of the Duat was reconciled by merging the two great deities. In the profoundest depths of the darkness, each god infused the other with his revitalizing powers and the two embraced to become one, a god referred to as "Ra in Osiris, Osiris in Ra".

Details of the sun god's nightly journey are found in three great funerary texts, *The Book of Amduat*, *The Book of Caverns* and *The Book of Gates,* and are also portrayed in royal tombs. Each hour of the night was regarded as a separate region or cavern, each with its own gateway guarded by a host of demigods and demons. In order for Ra and his divine retinue (and deceased mortals who made the same journey) to pass through the underworld safely, they had to possess a complete knowledge

THE SACRED SCARAB

The Egyptians chose the scarab, or dung beetle, to represent Khepri, the sun god at dawn. The image of Khepri propelling the sun out of the underworld and up into the skies derives from the way in which scarabs push balls of dung up from their burrows and propel them across the ground. The dung contains the beetle's larvae, which incubate within before breaking out and taking flight. For the Egyptians, this apparently miraculous act symbolized the sun god's powers of creation and self-generation, as reflected in the name Khepri (the "One who Came into Being").

As Atum-Khepri, the creator sun god arose on the primeval hill, imagery captured in a great stone scarab beetle erected by Amenhotep III beside the sacred lake at Karnak. On a smaller, more delicate scale, the jewelry of Tutankhamun includes several scarabs propelling the sun disc, an image that simultaneously represents eternal life and spells out one of the king's names: Nebkheperure ("Lordly Manifestation of Ra"). Generally portrayed as a scarab, Khepri can also be portrayed as a man with a head in the form of a beetle.

Shu separates Nut, the sky, and Geb, the earth. After travelling along the underside of Nut's body by day, the sun is swallowed by the goddess each evening and passes through her body with the stars during the night, to be reborn at sunrise. The red dawn sky represents Nut's blood as she gives birth to the sun.

of the guardians' names and powers. Ra subdued them by the simple but potent act of uttering their names. For example, on entering the first cavern, he declared: "Stinger in your cavern, Frightening One! Submit and give way!" As Ra passed from one cavern to the next, his enemies were mercilessly slaughtered. Ra's daughter, the Eye, "thrust her spear into Apophis", and Seth was also depicted spearing the serpent from the prow of the night barque. Finally, Apophis was skewered by knives, tied in knots and rendered "eyeless, noseless and earless". At the same time, the blessed dead who dwelled in the underworld were nightly revived by the god's life-giving light.

After successfully passing through the 12th and final gate, Ra prepared to emerge back into the world. Taking the form of Khepri, the scarab beetle, he was raised aloft in his barque by the primeval waters of Nun, while the sky goddess Nut reached down to support him, Nut in turn being supported by Osiris in the underworld. However, the sun god was more often described as being reborn directly from the womb of Nut, appearing amid the blood of childbirth indicated by the red of the eastern sky at dawn. The idea that the sun god travelled through the body of Nut by night (see illustration on page 47) incorporated the concept of his voyage through Duat, because the Egyptians conceived Duat simultaneously as an underworld and as a region within the body of the night sky.

The sun god had three main forms, as one text clearly sets out: "I am Khepri in the morning [see box on page 46], Ra at noon, Atum in the evening". However, the Egyptians succinctly captured every facet of the sun's powers through a wide range of solar gods. Supreme among them was Ra, whose name means simply "sun". Goddesses were described as "Mother of Ra" to enhance their status and male deities were regularly amalgamated with him in order to harness his awesome powers. Thus Amun became Amun-Ra, king of the gods (see pages 52–57), and other potent combinations included Khnum-Ra, Sobek-Ra and Ra-Atum. In the case of Ra-Atum, the sun god was combined with his own ancient creator aspect to represent the setting sun.

Ra rising at dawn could also be combined with Horakhty, an aspect of the falcon god Horus ("Horus of the Horizon"), to produce Ra-Horakhty. Another solar Horus form was Horemakhet ("Horus in the Horizon"). The Great Sphinx of Giza, created as an image of the Fourth-Dynasty pharaoh Khafra, was later reinterpreted as an image of Horemakhet, at whose feet each new pharaoh received the blessings of the sun god. Occasionally all forms of the sun god combined to give Ra-Horakhty-Atum-Horus-Khepri.

The sun disc in the sky was called the *aten* and was revered as the means by which the sun's light entered the world. During the 18th Dynasty it was elevated to the level of a deity. Amenhotep III (ruled ca. 1390–1352BCE) adopted the epithet "Dazzling Aten" and built the Aten its own temple at Heliopolis. Eventually the sun was predominantly worshipped in this form and absorbed the titles and attributes of many other gods. Under his son Amenhotep IV (ruled ca. 1352–1336BCE), who adopted the name Akhenaten ("Beneficial to the Aten"), the Aten became Egypt's supreme god, typically portrayed as a radiant sun disc, with each ray ending in a small hand holding an *ankh* symbol of life. However, Akhenaten initially worshipped the Aten as Ra-Horakhty, and depicted his god, like Ra and Horus, as a man with a falcon's head.

Various divine beings hail the rising sun, depicted as the solar disc or *aten*, the medium through which the sun god dispensed light and life to the world. The souls of dead kings were thought to "rise up and join with the *aten*". A detail from the sarcophagus lid of the royal scribe Nes-shutefnut, ca. 300BCE.

Akhenaten was not a monotheist, as has often been claimed. While Amun and his powerful priesthood were suppressed for political reasons, and Osiris and his dark realm were deemed to be incompatible with the light-filled theology of the Aten, Egypt's other traditional deities continued to be worshipped. A hymn found in five tombs at Amarna, the site of Akhenaten's capital of Akhetaten ("Horizon of the Aten"), mentions Ra-Horakhty, Shu, Maat and Ra, and one of Akhenaten's own titles, Neferkheperure, contains the names of the solar gods Ra and Khepri. Amun was reinstated as Egypt's supreme deity by Tutankhamun, but the Aten continued to be venerated as one aspect of the great sun god for several more reigns.

DIVINE BEINGS

At the heart of Egypt's religion were its many gods and goddesses, the actors in a great body of stories and myths, who also protected the dead on their journey into the afterlife. Venerated in huge temples and domestic shrines, these divinities could take many forms and were portrayed as humans or animals or a hybrid of both. The identities of gods and goddesses were often blurred, which explains how the sun god could unite with Amun to form Amun-Ra, while Isis and Hathor, for example, could be aspects of each other.

THE HIDDEN GOD

When Egypt was the greatest power of the ancient world, Amun was its greatest god. From a relatively minor role as one of the eight creator gods of the Ogdoad (see pages 14–15), Amun evolved through a complex pattern of myth to become Egypt's supreme deity, worshipped at the massive temple of Karnak in Thebes, Egypt's greatest city (see box below). He is first mentioned in the Old Kingdom *Pyramid Texts*, where the deceased king rises up to sit on the "throne of Amun", and he also occasionally appears in the *Coffin Texts* of the Middle Kingdom. Amun's powers were significantly enhanced during the New Kingdom, when he was amalgamated

KARNAK

From its origins at least as early as the Middle Kingdom, the temple of Amun at Karnak grew to become the largest and wealthiest religious centre in the ancient world. At times, the power of Karnak's influential priesthood came to rival even that of the

pharaoh. In the New Kingdom, as successive kings expanded Egypt's empire, they also enlarged and enriched the temple of the god to whom they attributed their success. Tuthmosis III (ruled ca. 1479–1425BCE) recorded the extensive conquests "given to him by his father Amun" on the sixth of Karnak's ten great pylons (ceremonial gateways), and Karnak was also greatly embellished by his predecessor, Hatshepsut, who set up a pair of gold-tipped red granite obelisks in front of the fourth pylon "for her father Amun" and called them "Amun Great in Majesty".

At Karnak, Amun was provided with a consort, Mut (see page 72), and a son, Khonsu, who both had their own temples in the complex. The three deities were worshipped as the "Theban Triad".

This detail from the pharaoh's *sed* (jubilee) pavilion at Karnak shows Sesostris (Senwosret) I before the fertility god Min, who was regarded as the ithyphallic aspect of Amun.

with the great sun god Ra to create Amun-Ra, "King of the Gods" and "Lord of the Thrones of the Two Lands".

Generally shown in human form with blue skin of lapis lazuli and wearing a characteristic tall plumed crown, Amun could also be represented by his sacred animals, the ram and the goose. As Amun Kamutef ("Bull of his Mother") he is pictured as a bull, while as Amun Kem-Atef ("He who has Completed his Moment"), he took the form of a serpent. However, despite his many guises, Amun was an unseen god – his name probably means "Hidden One" – and alone of all the gods he was ultimately regarded as unknowable. Yet he was all-pervading and, according to one temple inscription, existed "in the atmosphere at the end of the sky's circuit".

The cult of Amun developed in Thebes, and as the royal city grew in importance so too did Amun, Karnak and the theology associated with him. But Amun was also a popular god, to whom people could appeal directly outside the formal worship of the temples. Ordinary Egyptians regularly prayed to Amun, who is described in one New Kingdom papyrus as "Amun the compassionate, who listens to those who call." Nebra, a Theban workman, set up an inscription that declares: "Amun-Ra, Lord of the Thrones of the Two Lands, when I call out to you in distress you come and rescue me". In many ways Amun was regarded as a shepherd of his people, watching over them even when they travelled, in his guise of "Amun of the Road". With his worship came a sense of individual moral responsibility, since the god was also a judge – "Amun-Ra, who speaks to the heart, who judges the guilty".

THE GREAT HYMN TO AMUN

The most detailed surviving account of Amun is to be found in *The Great Hymn to Amun*, recorded in 18th-Dynasty papyri from Thebes. In it, the Theban priesthood attempted to express the very essence of a god who by definition was hidden and beyond human understanding. His identification with other deities is stressed, particularly with Ra, and his contribution to the creation myth is magnified to the extent that he becomes sole creator of the universe.

"Praise to Amun-Ra,
   Bull of Iunu [Heliopolis],
   chief of all the gods,
   the good god,
   the beloved one,
   who gives life to all!

Hail to you, Amun-Ra,
   Lord of the Thrones of the Two Lands,
   who rules in Thebes!
   Greatest of heaven,
   oldest on earth,
   Lord of All that Exists,
   who lives in all things. ...

Lord of Truth,
   father of the gods,
   who created humans and animals,
   Lord of All that Exists,
   who created the fruit trees,
   who made the green herbs and sustains the cattle,
   who made those below and those above.

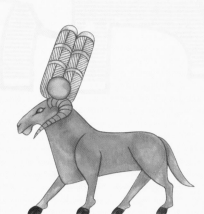

The gods fall at his feet,
knowing he is lord,
mighty in appearance!
Praise to you who created the gods,
raised up the sky and spread out the earth!
Awaken, Amun-Min,
Lord of Eternity, who created eternity,
praised one, presiding over the Ennead! …

Lord of the Rays, who creates light,
to whom all gods give praise,
who gives his hands to those whom he loves
and hurls his foes to the flames!
He hears the prayers of the prisoners,

is kind to those who call him,
rescues the frightened from their oppressors,
judges between the weak and the strong. …

Falcon in the midst of the horizon,
Lord of the Silent Ones,
whose name is hidden from his children
in his name of Amun,
Lord of Perception,
in whose mouth is authority!

You are the Only One who made all that is,
the One and the Only who made all that is,
from whose two eyes humankind issued,

from whose mouth the gods came into being.
He who made grass for the cattle,
fruit trees for humankind,
food for the fish in the river
and for the birds in the skies;
he gives breath to that which is in the egg
and to the offspring of worms,
he made food for the gnats,
for the worms and the flies,
for the mice in their holes
and for the birds in the trees.
Praise to you who did all this,
the Unique One with the many hands,
who never sleeps when humans sleep,

doing the best for all his creatures,
Amun, who lives in all things!

All praise to you who weary yourself for us,
all reverence for you because you created us!
'Praise you!' says every creature,
'Praise you!' says every wilderness,
to the heights of heaven,
to the ends of the earth,
to the depths of the great green sea! ...

Praise to you Amun-Ra,
Lord of the Thrones of the Two Lands,
whose arising his city adores!"

The Great Hymn to Amun

OSIRIS, LORD OF LIFE

The story of Osiris and Isis was possibly the most important Egyptian legend. It begins with the creation of the universe and ends with the invention of mummification, weaving together several strands of myth to explain the human condition and the existence of death; the generation of new life from death in an eternal cycle; the interaction of the divine and human worlds; and the succession of each pharaoh in a line of descent from the gods. The story can be traced back to the creation myth of Heliopolis (see pages 10–13), which the sun god's priesthood skilfully adapted to include – and subordinate – the increasingly significant cult of Osiris.

Following the world's dramatic beginnings, the sun god's children Shu and Tefnut produced Geb and Nut, who in turn produced Osiris, Isis, Seth and Nephthys. Born near Memphis, Osiris (Woser in Egyptian) was the eldest of the four and inherited the kingship of the earth from Geb. Under the rule of Osiris and Isis, his sister and consort, humankind was blessed with peace and prosperity. However, Seth was jealous of their good fortune and plotted to kill Osiris and seize the throne. Egyptian texts tend to be reti-

Osiris is depicted here with his royal emblems of crook, flail and *atef* (plumed crown). His skin is green, the colour of new vegetation, and represents fertility and regeneration. The myths of Osiris explained both the existence of death and the way in which new life arose from death. A wall painting from the Theban tomb of King Horemheb (ruled ca. 1319–1292BCE).

cent in describing the murder, saying simply that Osiris had "fallen on his side" or drowned. But according to the Greco-Roman version by Plutarch (second century CE), Seth tricked Osiris into trying out a fine new coffin. Once he was inside, Seth sealed the lid and hurled the coffin into the Nile. Thus Osiris drowned at the hand of his brother, and death and conflict entered the world. According to the *Coffin Texts*, the death of Osiris took place at Nedyet, near Abydos, the site of his greatest temple.

Isis retrieved the body, but Seth seized it again, dismembered it and scattered the parts all over Egypt – which explained how Osiris had so many important temples, each claiming to stand on the spot where a part of the god had been found. Abydos claimed his head, Athribis his heart and Sebennytos, Edfu and Biga all claimed his legs. Herakleopolis laid claim to his head, legs, and two sides. Isis found her husband's

THE LORD OF FERTILITY

The restoration to life of Osiris explains his role as the god of agricultural fertility. Egyptians attributed to Osiris, the first being to experience the cycle of life, death and resurrection, the miraculous way in which vegetation constantly renewed itself from its own seed. *The Great Hymn to Osiris* (see page 61) declares that "plants sprout at his command," and he can be portrayed as a prone mummiform figure with crops growing from his form. One inscription hails Osiris as the "Great One on the Riverbanks" and "Maker of the Grain", and he can be depicted either with black skin representing the fertile Nile mud or with green skin representing the crops that grow there.

To harness Osiris's regenerative powers and assist their own rebirth in the underworld, Egyptians were often buried with "Osiris Beds", wooden trays in the shape of the god and filled with soil and seeds. The germination of the seeds reflected the way in which, it was hoped, the deceased would similarly reemerge from death.

penis at Memphis, although according to a later tradition Seth threw it into the river, where it was eaten by fish, and Isis had to fashion a false one.

After Isis and her sister Nephthys had tracked down every piece of the corpse, it was reassembled and embalmed with the aid of the jackal god Anubis to create the first mummy. Using her immense magical powers, Isis revived Osiris for long enough for her to conceive their son Horus, whom she raised in secret to avenge his father.

Osiris then left the earth to become the ruler of the underworld, or Duat. As such, one of his principal tasks was to judge the souls of the dead and determine whether they should be granted an eternal, blissful afterlife (see pages 124–129). This helps to explain why Osiris was so popular among the Egyptians. To aid them on the hazardous journey through the Duat (see pages 116–121), they identified themselves with Isis, Horus and Osiris, the three deities who represented the defeat of evil and life after death. The most important was Osiris, the god of resurrection, and in funerary writings the name "Osiris" is prefixed to the deceased's own name in order to invoke the god's power in his or her quest for immortality.

The *Pyramid Texts* place Osiris in the heavens, but he was generally said to reside in the Duat, described in *The Book of the Dead* as "totally deep, totally dark, totally eternal". The utter blackness of his realm was penetrated only by the brilliance of the sun god Ra on his nightly journey (see pages 45–46).

The deceased, a man called Wepetmose, prays to Osiris (centre, left) and Ra-Horakhty on this early 19th-Dynasty stela. Osiris is shown as a mummy with his hands protruding from his wrappings to grasp his royal staff and flail.

THE GREAT HYMN TO OSIRIS

The most complete account of the death and resurrection of Osiris to date from the dynastic period of Egyptian history is to be found in *The Great Hymn to Osiris*. Composed in typically allusive language, this text was inscribed on a stela erected by a New Kingdom priest called Amenmose, Overseer of the Cattle of Amun at Thebes, and his wife Nefertari. The following is an extract:

"Placed on his father's throne,
Praised by his father Geb
Beloved of his mother Nut
Mighty as he kills the rebels,
Strong of arm when he kills his foe,
Spreading fear through his enemies,
Vanquishing the evildoers,
Crushing the rebels with steady heart ...

His sister is his guard:
Driving off his foes,
She stops the disturber

By the power of her words.
The clever-tongued one
Whose speech never fails,
Mighty Isis, protector of her brother!
Who sought him unwearying,
Who roamed the land mourning,
Not resting until she found him.
Making shade with her plumage,
Creating breath with her wings,
She rejoiced and joined with him,
Raising his inertia,
Receiving his seed to bear the heir."

ISIS, MISTRESS OF MAGIC

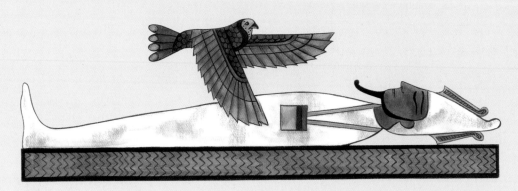

Isis hovers over the embalmed body of Osiris in the form of a kite. With her wings she fans him with the "breath of life", restoring him to life for long enough to conceive their son Horus.

A striking aspect of the story of Osiris and Isis is the way in which Osiris is largely passive while Isis takes the more active role, restoring her dead brother and husband to life by means of her magic. Egyptians revered Osiris as the being through whom life after death became possible, but they were also in awe of the goddess who possessed the mighty power to resurrect the dead. Known as the "Mistress of Magic" and "the clever-tongued one whose speech never fails", Isis was reckoned "more powerful than a thousand soldiers" and "more clever than a million gods". Her name (Aset in Egyptian) means "throne", the symbol she wears as a sign of her power.

Following the murder of Osiris by Seth, Isis made Osiris's body whole again (see page 60) and revived him with her magic. Taking the shape of a bird of prey (a kite) and miraculously "raising his inertia", as *The Great Hymn to Osiris* succinctly puts it, she conceived Horus. To conceal the infant from Seth, Isis took him deep into the marshes of the Delta to raise him "in solitude, his abode known by none" (*Great Hymn to Osiris*). Outwitting Seth through a potent combination of her wits and magic, she brought Horus to manhood so that he might avenge his father's death and reclaim the throne that was rightfully his (see pages 64–67).

Isis was regarded by Egyptians as the archetypal mother figure and countless generations of Egyptian women prayed to her to watch over their children. As the doting mother of Horus, Isis was also the divine mother of every king, who was identified with Horus. In the end, the powers attributed to the goddess became so great that by Roman times Isis had come to be regarded as the most powerful of all Egyptian deities. Her cult spread far beyond Egypt, and there were temples to Isis on three continents. Isis vied for popularity with Christianity, but in the end it was the new religion that triumphed. However, the last temple of Isis, at Philae in the far south of Egypt, was still functioning as late as ca. 535CE – a century and a half after the Romans had decreed the closure of all non-Christian places of worship in the empire. It is widely believed that the classic Christian image of the Madonna and Child probably derives ultimately from late Egyptian representations of Isis suckling the infant Horus.

ISIS AND NEPHTHYS

Isis and her faithful sister Nephthys were revered as protectors and restorers of the dead, and they were commonly depicted on coffins, with Isis at the feet of the deceased and Nephthys at the head. Generally represented in human guise, they can also be depicted as kites or as female figures with wings, with which they shaded and protected their brother Osiris as he was restored to life. Their protective role was especially important to the dead king, who was identified with Osiris, and the *Pyramid Texts* exhort the deceased monarch: "Raise yourself, as Osiris! Isis has your arm, Osiris, and Nephthys has your hand. So go between them."

A later text, *The Lamentations of Isis and Nephthys*, was recited as part of secret funeral rites by two priestesses who assumed the roles of the goddesses in the story of Osiris. Isis declares: "Gods and men all search for you, they weep for you together! While I can see I call to you, crying out to heaven, but you do not hear me. Yet I am your sister whom you loved on earth, and you loved none but me, your sister." Nephthys rejoins: "Good king, come to your house, be happy! All your foes are gone, your two sisters are beside you, they guard your bier and call out to you through their tears. I am Nephthys, your beloved sister, I am with you, your bodyguard for all eternity."

HORUS AND SETH

One of the most important Egyptian deities, Horus is also one of the most complex. A falcon god hailed as "Lord of the Sky", whose wings stretched to the very limits of the heavens, his name (Har or Hor in Egyptian) seems to derive from the concept of being "high" or "far away". In the form of Horakhty ("Horus of the Horizon") and Horemakhet ("Horus in the Horizon", rendered in Greek as Harmachis), he is also associated with the rising sun. Horus was worshipped throughout Egypt, notably at Edfu and Hierakonpolis ("Hawk Town") in Upper Egypt and at Letopolis in the Delta. From the very beginning of Egyptian history he symbolized the

THE EYE OF HORUS

After Seth had gouged out Horus's eyes they were restored, in most accounts, by the goddess Hathor. Generally referred to in the singular, the Eye of Horus came to symbolize the process of healing and the concept of making something whole and perfect again – the Egyptian name for the Eye is *wedjat* or *udjat*, meaning "sound, whole". *Wedjat* eyes were regarded as powerful amulets and in the form of jewelry they often adorned the neck and wrists of both the living and the dead. They appear on the sides of Middle Kingdom coffins to protect the deceased and to allow him or her to see out. The Eye's characteristic outline combines the markings of a falcon's eye with an extended cosmetic line of the sort applied by Egyptians with either kohl or malachite eyepaint, which was green and symbolic of new life. The Eye of Horus was such a potent force it even had its own priesthood.

In some myths, Horus's eyes represent the sun and moon, held aloft by the great falcon god as he flies through the skies. In his capacity as a lunar god, Thoth can be depicted holding out the Left Eye of Horus (the moon). It was said that the left eye had been more seriously damaged than the right, which explained why the sun was brighter than the moon.

A magnificent crowned hawk's head representing Horus, discovered at the god's temple at Hierakonpolis (ancient Nekhen). It is made of gold with eyes formed from a single rod of obsidian and dates from the Old Kingdom (6th Dynasty, ca. 2350–2170BCE).

divine nature of kingship, with each successive pharaoh hailed as the "Living Horus", while his dead predecessor was identified with Osiris, the father of Horus.

After raising Horus in the Delta, Isis took him before a divine tribunal headed by the god Geb. The tribunal welcomed Horus and decided that the kingship, brutally usurped by Seth, was rightfully his. *The Memphite Theology* (see page 17) says that the gods initially decreed that Horus and Seth should share the kingdom, but this solution failed so they eventually declared in favour of Horus alone. But Seth did not give up the throne without a fight, and the dispute between the two gods is related in a lively and indeed violent account from the Ramesside era (19th and 20th Dynasties) known as *The Contendings of Horus and Seth*. In this version, the divine tribunal is led by the sun god Ra, who prefers the older and more experienced Seth, "great of strength", over the youthful Horus. Thoth writes to the creator goddess Neith for advice and she angrily replies that unless Horus is given the throne she will cause the sky to crash down. But Ra remains doubtful and asks Horus and Seth each to plead his case before the divine tribunal.

The skilled advocacy of "clever-tongued" Isis wins her son increasing sympathy and Seth becomes so angry he threatens to kill one god a day unless they eject Isis from the court. They do so, but Isis returns in disguise and, by a trick, gets Seth to condemn his usurpation of the throne before the whole court.

However, the feud continues. Later, Isis sees Seth suffering and takes pity on him, prompting Horus to fly into a murderous rage in which he beheads her with his knife and flees into the desert. Having now enraged the gods, and without his mother to guard him, Horus is easy prey for Seth, who attacks him and rips out his eyes – but

The gods Horus (left) and Anubis greet the soul of the deceased pharaoh in this scene from the tomb of King Ramses I (ruled ca. 1292–1290BCE) in the Valley of the Kings. The falcon-headed Horus wears the double crown representing the union of Egypt's "Two Lands".

not before Horus has torn off Seth's testicles. Thoth restores the head of Isis while Hathor tends to Horus, restoring his sight with the milk of a gazelle. Seth, also restored, plans to rape Horus – a humiliation that would show Seth's superiority once and for all. Isis, now reconciled with her son, warns him to catch Seth's semen in his hands. After the attack, Horus gives the semen to his mother, who throws it into a ditch. She then takes some of Horus's own semen and sprinkles it over Seth's favourite lettuce plants, which the unsuspecting Seth eats.

Seth announces to the tribunal that he has "done a man's deed" to Horus and demands the throne. The Ennead laugh at Horus and are about to declare in Seth's favour when Horus asks Thoth to arbitrate by calling forth each god's semen. To Seth's shock, his semen is found to be far away in a ditch, but Horus's turns out to be within Seth. The tribunal denounces Seth as "effeminate" and unfit to rule.

Despite this humiliation Seth refuses to give in and he challenges Horus to a boat race using stone ships. Horus wins by disguising his wooden ship as a stone one, but Seth turns himself into a raging hippopotamus and rams Horus's boat. Horus is about to spear his rival when the gods intervene to prevent him.

Meanwhile, Thoth writes to Osiris, who inevitably finds in favour of his son. He threatens to unleash a cataclysm on the earth that would bring everything down into the underworld, gods and all, unless Horus is given the throne. The divine tribunal at last unites in deciding that Horus must be made king. After eight decades of conflict, Seth is finally defeated and given over to Isis as her prisoner. *The Contendings of*

Horus and Seth ends with the words of Isis: "The entire land is in joy, as they see Horus, son of Isis, given the office of his father Osiris."

The inexperienced young god soon became a great king, hailed as "Strong-armed Horus, Lord of Action". He was the mythical prototype for every king, and his immediate successors were known as the "Followers of Horus", the name given to the semi-mythical earliest pharaohs in one list of kings. Seth's ultimate defeat symbolized the triumph of order over chaos. Throughout Egyptian history, the pharaoh – the Living Horus – was depicted smiting his enemy or spearing fierce wild beasts associated with Seth such as the oryx, donkey, boar and hippopotamus. Such images adorn the great temple of Horus at Edfu, where the ritual spearing of Seth was performed as a sacred drama each year in commemoration of the triumph of justice and order.

SETH THE MIGHTY

Seth was associated with chaos, disruption, storms, thunder, the desert, foreign lands, redheads and antisocial behaviour. "Seth is the god within him", says one papyrus of a man who cannot contain his drinking, lust or temper. Depicted as a strange beast with a pointed snout and squared ears (right), Seth displayed his turbulent nature at birth when he tore himself from Nut's womb at Naqada. Yet Seth cannot be dismissed as "evil", for his presence was seen as an essential counterweight to the order represented by Horus. After Horus's victory, the sun god placed Seth at the prow of his barque to combat the true forces of darkness. Many venerated Seth for his great strength, notably the 19th- and 20th-Dynasty kings, some of whom bore his name (Set in Egyptian). Seth had temples at Naqada and in the eastern Delta.

DAUGHTERS OF RA

A number of important goddesses could claim descent from the great sun god. First among them was Maat, goddess of truth, justice and cosmic harmony, whom the creator god brought into being at the beginning of time to stabilize the workings of the universe (see page 19). Equally vital to Ra's existence was his daughter Hathor, who protected him and was likewise present in his great solar barque, "the beautiful face in the boat of the millions". Originally known as Bat, Hathor was most often associated with a cow, and first appeared in bovine form in Predynastic times. Hathor is frequently represented as a woman wearing a crown of cow horns, with the sun disc set between them to show her relationship with her father Ra and her role as "Lady of the Sky". Usually referred to as a goddess of love, beauty and sensual pleasures, her range of epithets included "Lady of Drunkenness", reflecting the quantities of wine consumed during her worship. She was also the patron of music and dancing.

Hathor's name derives from the Egyptian Huwt-Har, literally "House of Horus", apparently an allusion to her womb, which contained and protected Horus. It was not at all unusual for a deity to claim more than one divine father or mother, and Hathor shares her role as mother of Horus with Isis. Isis too was linked with cows: as the mother of the sacred Apis bull (see pages 76–77) she was hailed as

Among the number of female deities depicted in bovine form was Mehetweret, a goddess of the heavens. On a gilded couch from the tomb of Tutankhamun (left), she is portrayed almost identically to Hathor, with a solar disc between her horns. The stars on a Predynastic image of the cow goddess Bat (opposite page) reflect her celestial associations.

"Mother of Apis" and worshipped in the guise of the Isis cow, a sacred animal that received state burial in the Iseum at Sakkara. Since the king was equated with Horus, Hathor too was regarded as the mother of the king. Egyptian religion was flexible and all-embracing and a goddess could combine the role of mother, wife and daughter of the same god. As her mythology evolved, Hathor was also described as Horus's wife, and to emphasize the cyclical nature of all things she was referred to as both the daughter and mother of Ra.

Hathor was frequently invoked in private tombs, as in this inscription from the tomb of May, a Theban harbour-master of the 18th Dynasty: "We are drunk at the sight of your beautiful face, Golden Hathor!" As "Lady of the West" Hathor resided in the western hills and received the souls of the dead, and she is often portrayed as a cow emerging from the Theban cliffs to welcome the deceased into the afterlife.

Hathor and Isis, Egypt's greatest and most popular mother goddesses, became so closely associated as to be virtually indistinguishable. Eventually, Hathor was subsumed into the great international cult of Isis (see page 63).

Hathor represented not only the gentle, caring and protective side of female nature, symbolized by the cow, but also its fiery, unpredictable side. In her protective capacity she was also referred to as the Eye of Ra, in which guise she took the form of the fearsome lioness goddess Sekhmet ("Powerful One"), who brought death to all those who opposed her father (see page 12). A Greco-Roman hymn from Edfu declares: "Sekhmet, Eye of Ra! Lady of protection for her creator! Sekhmet, fill the ways with blood! Slaughtering to the limits all she sees". Sekhmet's power was invoked by the king, with one papyrus describing Sesostris III (ruled ca. 1874–1855 BCE) as "a Sekhmet against his enemies". Queens were also likened to Sekhmet as protectors of their royal husbands. Tiy, the formidable consort of the great Amenhotep III (ruled ca. 1391–1354BCE), was depicted as a rampaging lioness trampling her husband's enemies, and the military exploits of Queen Ahhotep (ca. 1590–1530BCE) were so great it was said she must be "united with the limbs of Sekhmet".

Sekhmet was regarded as the consort of the creator god Ptah, and like him she was associated with the ancient capital of Memphis in Lower Egypt. Her regional links to the red crown are reflected in her epithet "Lady of Red Linen", which also alludes to the blood of her slaughtered foes. Sekhmet was the bringer of pestilence, and her priests therefore functioned as doctors. She travelled through the sky in the barque of Ra, helping him to fend off his enemies on his nightly voyage through the underworld.

The same leonine symbolism could extend to Tefnut, goddess of moisture, whom the sun god produced along with her twin brother Shu in the solar creation myth of

THE LION IN NUBIA

In the leonine form of Tefnut, the Eye of Ra takes centre stage in a myth preserved in a late papyrus. After quarrelling with her father, the sun god, over his attempts to curb her powers (see pages 12–13), the volatile Eye left Egypt and travelled south into Nubia, where she lived in self-imposed exile.

Without his Eye, Ra's powers were seriously diminished and order was hopelessly disrupted throughout the land. It was essential that the goddess return to him, yet no one dared to use force against her. Instead Shu, her twin brother and partner, was sent out as Ra's envoy, taking the name Onuris, which means "He who Brings Back the Far One". To facilitate her return journey, the god Thoth won her over by entertaining her with stories, and by the time she arrived back in Egypt her rage had diminished to the extent that the raging lioness had become a contented domesticated cat – the benign and gentle Bastet (see main text).

A gold and turquoise pectoral in the form of the vulture goddess Nekhbet, discovered in the royal tombs of the 21st Dynasty (ca. 1075–945BCE) at Tanis in the Delta. Her wings are outstretched in a protective embrace and in her talons she clutches *shen* signs, meaning "eternity" and "protection".

Heliopolis (see pages 10–11). Both Shu and Tefnut were worshipped as a pair of lions, and their relationship was extended to the king and queen. For example, Amenhotep III's identification with Shu was complemented by the representation of his wife Tiy as Tefnut. Like Sekhmet, Tefnut was regarded as the Eye of Ra (see box opposite), and she was worshipped at the sun god's centre of Heliopolis. In fact, Tefnut's lioness form blurs with Sekhmet, whose destructive powers she shares.

Another feline deity is the cat goddess Bastet, whose name means "She of the Perfume Jar" and perhaps refers to the ritual purity involved in her worship, which was based at Bubastis in the Delta. Capable of ferocity when defending her father Ra, and invoked for protective purposes in the *Coffin Texts*, Bastet was more usually regarded as a gentle and amiable deity, perfectly personified by the cats the Egyptians were so fond of (see page 74).

Two foreign goddesses were incorporated into the Egyptian pantheon as daughters of the sun god Ra. The Syrian war deities Anat and Astarte both have characteristics which were merged with those of Hathor, who was associated with foreign lands and like them had a distinctly violent streak. Anat was referred to as "Lady of the Sky" and Astarte was portrayed with a head dress of cow horns. In *The Contendings of Horus*

A blue faience hippopotamus dating from the Middle Kingdom. It represents Taweret, who was invoked to ward off evil, especially during childbirth.

and Seth (see pages 64–67), the creator goddess Neith advises Ra to console Seth for his failure by presenting him with the two war goddesses as his consorts.

Almost all the goddesses of Egypt were associated with fertility and childbirth. This is most graphically represented by the sky goddess Nut creating each new day by giving birth to the sun god amid the blood-red glow of dawn, an eternal cycle of rebirth to which the dead appealed, as in this invocation to Nut in the *Coffin Texts*: "May you conceive me in the night, to give birth to me every morning, like Ra every day."

Neith (see page 17) was credited with having introduced the actual process of birth. She was a nurturing goddess, always ready to support her divine offspring. In *The Lamentations of Isis and Nephthys*, Nephthys tells her brother Osiris to "come and see your mother Neith, come to her overflowing breasts".

The Theban goddess Mut also plays a prominent maternal role, unsurprisingly since her name means "mother". A late sacred text describes her as "the mother of mothers, who gave birth to every god", and she was regarded as another of the divine mothers of the king. As the consort of Amun, Mut is the mother of Khonsu; the temples of Mut and Khonsu formed part of Amun's sacred complex at Karnak.

Mut also means "vulture" and she was generally represented as a woman wearing a vulture headdress of a kind that also came to be worn by Egyptian queens. She was closely associated with the far older deity Nekhbet, the vulture goddess of Upper Egypt venerated at Nekheb (el-Kab). Nekhbet also played a maternal role as a divine mother of the king from at least as early as the Old Kingdom, when she appears in the *Pyramid Texts* to suckle King Sahure: "The king knows his mother, the White Crown [Nekhbet], splendid and rounded, residing in Nekheb". Nekhbet can also take on the bovine guise of the "Great White Cow residing in Nekheb with the two tall plumes and the two swollen breasts".

Other deities who played a significant role in the birth process were Taweret, the hippopotamus goddess whose name means "the great one", and her male counterpart, the dwarf god Bes (sometimes referred to in his feminine guise as Beset). Their fearsome appearances, together with the knives and amulets they carried, scared away evil forces from around the home and protected women during the difficult and often life-threatening process of childbirth. So effective were their powers that pregnant women wore small amulets of Taweret and Bes during this difficult time, and images of the deities were placed in household shrines. They were also used more generally to decorate the house and its furnishings.

BIRTH RITUALS

Great precautions were taken both before and after the birth to ensure the health of both mother and child. Medical texts gave advice on diet – honey and fenugreek would "loosen the child in the womb", for example – and magical spells were recited. Hathor was asked to bring the cooling north wind to speed up the birth. Khnum made women "give birth when their wombs are ready" and Bes was invoked to "bring down the placenta". The mother squatted on bricks (right) to give birth, and her clothes and hair were loosened to ease the delivery. Other goddesses were called upon to be divine midwives, including Nekhbet, Taweret, Isis, Nephthys, Meskhenet (who personified the birthing-bricks) and Heket (a frog goddess). Following a successful delivery, the mother underwent 14 days of seclusion and purification. Further protective rituals for mother and baby were performed seven days after the birth.

ANIMAL SPIRITS

Most Egyptian deities were associated with at least one animal and almost every god could be represented as an animal or as a human with animal features. The animals linked with a particular deity featured prominently in his or her worship, but were not themselves the object of veneration – they were revered as manifestations of the deity or as embodiments of divine characteristics. Creatures associated with the gods ranged from birds, felines and cattle to reptiles, fish and even insects.

At least as early as ca. 5000BCE, the prehistoric inhabitants of the Nile Valley were depicting the animals which they hunted, domesticated and ultimately venerated, and

THE FESTIVAL OF THE CAT

Cats are perhaps the most familiar animals associated with Egyptian worship. While the sun god Ra could take the form of the great Solar Cat, the creatures were generally associated with his daughter Bastet, who was initially worshipped in the form of a lion but achieved her greatest popularity as a cat goddess. Her religious centre at Bubastis in the Delta achieved great notoriety for its raucous pilgrims, who greatly shocked the Greek writer Herodotus when he visited Egypt in the fifth century BCE. He wrote an account of the festival of Bastet in his *Histories*: "When the people travel to Bubastis they go by river, men and women together in great numbers in every boat. Some of the women make a noise with clappers, others play the oboe while the rest of the women and men sing and clap their hands. Throughout their journey down to Bubastis, whenever they come to a town, they bring their boat close to the bank. Some of the women shout mockery to the women of that town, while others dance and others stand up and expose their private parts! But when they reach Bubastis they hold a great festival, and more wine is drunk at this feast than in all the rest of the year."

A sunken relief sculpture on a column at the Greco-Roman temple of Horus and Sobek at Kom Ombo, near Aswan. It shows the vulture goddess Nekhbet (centre) wearing the *atef*, a plumed ritual crown, and a hierakosphinx (left), a creature with the head of a hawk and the body of a lion, wearing the crown of Upper and Lower Egypt.

the representation of animals continued throughout the pharaonic period, both in pictures and in hieroglyphic script. Perhaps the most frequently represented creatures were birds, which were associated with the gods in the heavens – especially birds of prey, soaring and hovering high in the sky yet scanning the ground far below with their keen eyes. The most important bird was the falcon, representing Ra and Horus, while Isis and Nephthys were described as kites and often shown with kite wings (see pages 62–63). The huge wingspan of the vulture goddess Nekhbet protected the king, who might wear Nekhbet's head on his crown alongside the cobra (uraeus). Protective plumage was incorporated into royal costume and wings and feather patterns also covered the coffins of the dead.

Among the waterfowl of the Nile, the ibis was connected with Thoth and the grey heron came to be identified with the *benu* bird of Ra (see page 45). Geese were linked with two of the mightiest gods, Geb and Amun. In his creative aspect, Amun was associated with the "Great Honker", the primordial goose whose cry was the first noise in the universe, breaking the primeval silence and initiating the creation of life.

Cats and large felines were a great source of inspiration, associated most notably with Bastet (see box opposite) and Sekhmet (see pages 69–70), whose regional forms included Pakhet ("Scratcher"). Both Shu and Tefnut could be portrayed as a pair of lions, as could the earth god Aker (see page 29). Lions inhabited desert margins and hence were considered to be guardians of the sun on the eastern and western horizons.

Fierce power was also displayed by the crocodiles which once proliferated along the

Nile (see box opposite). Even fish were believed to contain something of the divine essence. The Oxyrynchus fish was said in one account to have swallowed the phallus of Osiris after it had been thrown into the river by Seth. Hatmehyt ("Leader of Fish") was a fish goddess worshipped at Mendes in the Delta, and a fish sacred to Hathor was the tilapia, whose habit of hiding its young in its mouth to protect them and then spitting them out symbolized regeneration. The frog goddess Heket was a deity of childbirth for a similar reason – the abundance of young spawned by frogs.

Snakes could represent both order and chaos. The embodiment of evil was the terrifying serpent Apophis, which dwelt in the underworld and had the potential to devour the sun god on his nightly journey. However, four of the creator deities of the Ogdoad took the form of snakes, and gods such as Amun Kematef, Osiris and Hathor could also sometimes appear in serpentine form. The snake god Nehebkau and the snake goddesses Wadjyt, Renenutet and Meretseger were also protective deities.

Just as cows were associated with powerful goddesses to emphasize their nurturing roles (see pages 68–70), bulls were linked with male gods. Living bulls were the focus of three important cults, each animal being selected on account of characteristics that marked it out as the creature containing the spirit (*ba*) of a god. The Apis bull of Memphis was associated with Ptah, the Buchis bull of Armant with Montu and the Mnevis bull of Heliopolis with Ra. As symbols of virility,

A worshipper kneels before the Apis bull on this Late Period painted limestone stela from the Serapeum at Sakkara, where the mummified bodies of the bulls were entombed. Believed to contain the spirit of Ptah, the Apis bull was worshipped at nearby Memphis and its death was a time of national mourning.

Nile (see box opposite). Even fish were believed to contain something of the divine essence. The Oxyrynchus fish was said in one account to have swallowed the phallus of Osiris after it had been thrown into the river by Seth. Hatmehyt ("Leader of Fish") was a fish goddess worshipped at Mendes in the Delta, and a fish sacred to Hathor was the tilapia, whose habit of hiding its young in its mouth to protect them and then spitting them out symbolized regeneration. The frog goddess Heket was a deity of childbirth for a similar reason – the abundance of young spawned by frogs.

Snakes could represent both order and chaos. The embodiment of evil was the terrifying serpent Apophis, which dwelt in the underworld and had the potential to devour the sun god on his nightly journey. However, four of the creator deities of the Ogdoad took the form of snakes, and gods such as Amun Kematef, Osiris and Hathor could also sometimes appear in serpentine form. The snake god Nehebkau and the snake goddesses Wadjyt, Renenutet and Meretseger were also protective deities.

Just as cows were associated with powerful goddesses to emphasize their nurturing roles (see pages 68–70), bulls were linked with male gods. Living bulls were the focus of three important cults, each animal being selected on account of characteristics that marked it out as the creature containing the spirit (*ba*) of a god. The Apis bull of Memphis was associated with Ptah, the Buchis bull of Armant with Montu and the Mnevis bull of Heliopolis with Ra. As symbols of virility,

A worshipper kneels before the Apis bull on this Late Period painted limestone stela from the Serapeum at Sakkara, where the mummified bodies of the bulls were entombed. Believed to contain the spirit of Ptah, the Apis bull was worshipped at nearby Memphis and its death was a time of national mourning.

A sunken relief sculpture on a column at the Greco-Roman temple of Horus and Sobek at Kom Ombo, near Aswan. It shows the vulture goddess Nekhbet (centre) wearing the *atef*, a plumed ritual crown, and a hierakosphinx (left), a creature with the head of a hawk and the body of a lion, wearing the crown of Upper and Lower Egypt.

the representation of animals continued throughout the pharaonic period, both in pictures and in hieroglyphic script. Perhaps the most frequently represented creatures were birds, which were associated with the gods in the heavens – especially birds of prey, soaring and hovering high in the sky yet scanning the ground far below with their keen eyes. The most important bird was the falcon, representing Ra and Horus, while Isis and Nephthys were described as kites and often shown with kite wings (see pages 62–63). The huge wingspan of the vulture goddess Nekhbet protected the king, who might wear Nekhbet's head on his crown alongside the cobra (uraeus). Protective plumage was incorporated into royal costume and wings and feather patterns also covered the coffins of the dead.

Among the waterfowl of the Nile, the ibis was connected with Thoth and the grey heron came to be identified with the *benu* bird of Ra (see page 45). Geese were linked with two of the mightiest gods, Geb and Amun. In his creative aspect, Amun was associated with the "Great Honker", the primordial goose whose cry was the first noise in the universe, breaking the primeval silence and initiating the creation of life.

Cats and large felines were a great source of inspiration, associated most notably with Bastet (see box opposite) and Sekhmet (see pages 69–70), whose regional forms included Pakhet ("Scratcher"). Both Shu and Tefnut could be portrayed as a pair of lions, as could the earth god Aker (see page 29). Lions inhabited desert margins and hence were considered to be guardians of the sun on the eastern and western horizons.

Fierce power was also displayed by the crocodiles which once proliferated along the

Gilded and inset with lapis lazuli, four uraeus cobras rear up to protect the back of Tutankhamun's throne. The cobra represents Wadjyt, the goddess of Lower Egypt and counterpart of Nekhbet, the vulture goddess of Upper Egypt. In the royal titles they are called the "Two Ladies".

king was the high priest of every temple in Egypt, a role which for the most part he necessarily delegated to others. However, there were a number of important temple rites and ceremonies directly associated with the kingship and it was crucial that he perform these in person. The king therefore needed to be well versed in temple protocol and had to understand the great body of esoteric knowledge required for the secret rituals. A text from Luxor temple describes the role of Amenhotep III as high priest of Ra during rituals to greet the rising sun: "The king knows the secret words of the Souls of the East as they sing praises to Ra, as he rises at dawn. He knows their secret images, he knows their secret forms, he knows the place in which they stand, he knows the words spoken by those who drag forth the barque of the Horizon

The king's names contained many references to his relationships with the gods, serving as a constant reminder of his divine origins. The standard royal titulary consisted of five names, four of which referred to the deities Ra, Horus and the "Two Ladies" Wadjyt and Nekhbet. The epithet "Son of Ra", which always preceded the birth name (nomen), became "Daughter of Ra" (Sat Ra) in the case of female pharaohs such as Hatshepsut, who was also "Daughter of Amun".

In the balanced world of the Egyptians, it was only through the intervention of the king, the intermediary between the divine and human worlds, that order could triumph over the forces of chaos. This explains the frequent portrayal of the king smiting his enemy, hunting wild animals and offering a figure of Maat, the goddess of truth, to the gods to show how he maintained justice on earth on their behalf. The

RUDDEDET'S ROYAL TRIPLETS

The idea that the king was conceived by a god taking the form of his mortal father occurs throughout Egyptian history. The Westcar Papyrus, a Middle Kingdom document now in Berlin, tells how Userkaf, Sahura and Neferirkara, the first kings of the Fifth Dynasty, are fathered by Ra, in the guise of Rawoser, husband of Ruddedet. When her labour becomes difficult, Ra sends Isis, Nephthys, Meskhenet and Heket to deliver the three children "who will one day assume the kingship of the whole land". The goddesses set off disguised as itinerant dancers, with the god Khnum to carry their luggage. At the house of Ruddedet, they find Rawoser panic-stricken at his wife's pain. Pushing him aside, they lock themselves in the room with Ruddedet. With Isis in front, Nephthys behind and the others providing encouragement, Ruddedet gives birth to three healthy identical sons. Rawoser is so delighted he offers the goddesses a sack of barley "as payment for beer".

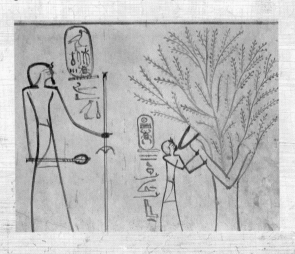

THE LIVING GOD

Occupying a unique position in the Egyptian universe was the king, or pharaoh (a Greek word derived from the Egyptian *per wer* meaning "great house" or "palace", which came to refer to its resident). From the beginning of Egyptian history he – or sometimes she – was regarded as the gods' representative on earth and their divine intermediary. The Egyptians regarded the kingship as having existed since the beginning of time. The *Pyramid Texts* describe the king as a primeval god "born in the waters of Nun before there was sky, before there were earth and mountains".

In Egypt's inclusive religious system, many deities were revered as the mother or father of the pharaoh. From as early as the Old Kingdom the king was referred to as "Son of Ra" (Sa Ra). In the earliest story relating to the divine conception of the king, Ra is said to be the father of the first three kings of the Fifth Dynasty, taking the form of their mortal father, the husband of Ruddedet (see box opposite). The later fusion of Amun with the ancient sun god meant that Amun-Ra came to be regarded as the true father of every pharaoh, and there are a number of New King-dom accounts of divine conception in which Amun-Ra adopts the physical form of the living king. In this way the god is said to have fathered the female pharaoh Hatshepsut (ruled ca. 1479–1458BCE) and the later monarchs Amenhotep III (ruled ca. 1390–1353BCE) and Ramses II (ruled ca. 1279–1213BCE). In his role as the "Living Horus", each reigning king was also regarded as the son of Osiris, who was identified with his deceased predecessor.

Amenhotep III, whose 37-year reign is viewed by many as the high point of ancient Egyptian civilization. In the account of his divine conception described and portrayed on the walls of the temple of Luxor, the god Amun-Ra adopts the guise of the king's father, Tuthmosis IV, and approaches his mother Mutemwia as she sleeps.

bulls were connected with ithyphallic gods such as Amun and Min. Rams were associated with Amun, Khnum and the Middle Egyptian ram god Heryshaf.

Canine deities included the jackal gods Anubis (Anpu), the guardian of burial grounds, and Wepwawet ("Opener of the Ways"), associated with Osiris. Dogs were used for hunting and were also kept as pets, as were cats and other creatures. Some went so far as to mummify their pets, but the vast majority of mummified animals were embalmed in an attempt to capture the animal's "spirit" and offer it back to the god with which it was associated. A huge range of creatures were mummified for this purpose, including crocodiles, lions, rats, vultures, ibises, cobras and even beetles. The mummies of falcons, ibises and cats have been discovered by the million – and destroyed by the million for fertilizer or fuel – and a cemetery of mummified lions still lies undiscovered beneath the sands of Memphis. Animals such as the Apis bulls died a natural death, but recent evidence has revealed that cats were sometimes strangled to order – surprisingly, given the apparent Egyptian fondness for these animals.

CROCODILES

Now extinct in Egypt owing to the Aswan Dam, crocodiles were a common sight in the Nile in ancient times, when they were personified by the fearsome god Sobek. The crocodile's ability to rise suddenly out of the water and attack its prey was likened to the might of the king, as expressed in the *Pyramid Texts*: "The king emerges from the primeval flood. He is Sobek the green, face ever watchful, brows uplifted". In *The Book of the Dead*, the god declares: "I am Sobek, who carries off by violence", and the book contains spells to protect the deceased from "crocodiles who eat the dead and live by magic". At his main centres of Kom Ombo in Upper Egypt and Crocodilopolis in the Fayuum, crocodiles sacred to Sobek lived in pools, decked out in golden jewelry and tended by the god's priesthood.

Dweller; he knows the manifestations of the sun god and all his forms."

A thousand years earlier, the king was viewed more as the servant of the gods than their equal on earth, as in this description of King Unas in the *Pyramid Texts*: "Unas is the steward of the god, behind the mansion of Ra. Unas squats before him and opens his boxes, Unas unseals his decrees and dispatches, and Unas does what Unas is told". However, it is also clear from the so-called *Cannibal Hymn* elsewhere in the *Pyramid Texts* that the king drew strength from the gods by eating them, perhaps referring to a much earlier time when such bloody rituals actually existed: "Unas eats men and feeds on gods. Their throats are cut for him, their entrails torn out for him, they are carved up for him and cooked in his cooking pots. Unas devours their magic … and nothing can harm him, for he has swallowed the wisdom of every god."

DIVINE PROTECTORS OF THE KING

As the child of the gods, the king could invoke all manner of deities to safeguard his royal person. Tuthmosis III refers in his military annals to Amun, Ra, Horakhty, Wadjyt, Isis and Nephthys, while Ramses II puts his faith in Ra, Montu, Seth, Baal, Atum and Amun. Among his protectors was an array of powerful female deities. Nekhbet and Wadjyt, the patron deities of Upper and Lower Egypt, appear on the front of the king's crowns and head-dresses as the vulture and cobra to defend him against his enemies (see illustration on opposite page and on page 37). Another protective pair were Isis and Nephthys, while the two Syrian warrior goddesses Anat and Astarte protected the king in combat – a role more generally ascribed to the ferocious Sekhmet and the mother goddess Neith, "who shall place all people of the entire earth beneath Pharaoh's feet".

At death the king passed into the embrace of a host of guardian goddesses, including his "sisters" Isis and Nephthys, who reached down to help him on his final journey; Hathor, who enfolded him within herself; and Nut, who shielded the king's body with her own.

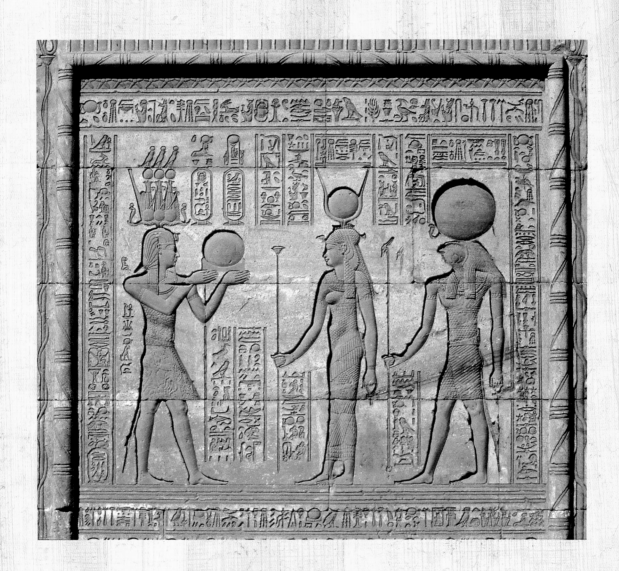

THE DANCE OF THE KING

The Egyptians believed that "song, dance and incense are nourishment for the gods".
All three played a part in the rituals that the king performed in honour of the gods
and goddesses, and this was especially true of Hathor, patron of music and dancing.
A hymn from her temple at Dendera describes how the king danced and sang for the
goddess, wielding a golden sistrum (see illustration on page 102) and fully attired in
Hathoric regalia, including the characteristic necklace called a *menat*:

"He comes to dance,
  comes to sing,
  Hathor, see his dancing,
  see his skipping!

He offers the jug to you,
Hathor, see his dancing,
see his skipping!

His heart is pure,
no evil in his body.
Hathor, see his dancing,
see his skipping!

O Golden One,
how fine is the song
like the song of Horus himself,
which Ra's son sings as the finest singer.
He is Horus, a musician!"

MYSTERIES OF THE TEMPLE

The temple was the junction of the human and divine worlds, the place where Egypt's gods and goddesses directed their powers to earth in return for a constant cycle of rites and offerings. A combination of church, town hall, college, library and clinic, the temple employed male and female clergy alongside scribes, musicians and many other specialists. But only the purified clergy could enter its inner precincts, where its holiest mysteries were hidden.

HOUSES OF THE GODS

An Egyptian temple was called *per netcher*, literally "house of god", referring to the divine spirit that resided within the cult statue in the temple's inner sanctuary. Around this holy shrine, the temple formed the stage on which a great array of daily rituals were performed in order to regulate the workings of the universe. Many temple rituals were based around processions and consequently the majority of Egypt's hundreds of temples were built along a straight axis. Most were aligned east-west, following the daily course of the sun.

As a storehouse of divine power, each temple was considered to embody the place at which creation had first occurred. A temple's ritual purpose dictated its architecture, and daily rituals reenacting the creation of the universe were greatly enhanced by a series of architectural "special effects". Open courts led to a series of increasingly smaller, darker chambers, and floor heights rose, ceilings became lower and doorways grew narrower as one approached the inner sanctuary. This stood on the highest

One of the best preserved Egyptian temples is that of Horus at Edfu in Upper Egypt. The extant remains are Ptolemaic but probably differ little in their general appearance from the more ancient structures that preceded them. The massive pylon (gateway) bears images of Ptolemy XII smiting enemies, and the long vertical niches that once held flagpoles can clearly be seen.

ground in the temple and represented the hill of creation (see page 11) – a symbolism enhanced by the way in which some temples seem to have been designed to allow the waters of the Nile inundation to flood certain areas.

Every part of the temple was decorated with images and texts appropriate to its function. On the massive exterior walls the king was portrayed destroying Egypt's enemies with the help of the gods. Inside walls displayed more tranquil and solemn scenes of the king presiding over an ordered world and honouring Egypt's divine protectors. Originally every surface would have been brightly painted and inlaid with a variety of precious materials to add further magical potency to each scene.

The great cult centre of Amun at Karnak (Ipet-sut) is generally regarded as the "classic" Egyptian temple. It originated ca. 2000BCE, when the Theban kings of the

FOUNDATION RITUALS

The building of each temple took place in several stages, each marked by an important ritual. At the foundation ceremony, called "Stretching the Cord", the king oversaw the delineation of the temple's outline on the ground. The ensuing rituals of "Hacking up the Ground", "Scattering the Sand" and "Placing the Bricks" aimed to ensure that the temple was built according to tradition. The homes of mortals – including the king – were usually built of mudbrick, but those of the gods were built in durable stone, with mudbrick only employed for the outer enclosure wall and subsidiary buildings. The finished temple was consecrated in a ceremony called "Handing over the Temple to its Lord". Special rites magically activated the hieroglyphs and ritual scenes that adorned the temple, thereby ensuring that they would be performed for eternity.

early Middle Kingdom set up a shrine to their local god, Amun, and from that time almost all of Egypt's rulers added to the temple in order to demonstrate their piety and outdo their predecessors. The main axis runs westward from the inner sanctuary containing Amun's cult statue to the Nile, a processional route along which the statue was carried during festivals. A second axis, running south, connects Amun's temple with the temple of his consort Mut. A third, smaller, temple honoured their son Khonsu.

Along each axis is a series of hypostyle (columned) halls, the most famous being that of Seti I (ruled ca. 1290–1279BCE), with its 134 huge papyrus-shaped columns – each standing 23 metres (77 feet) high – representing the primeval marshes of creation. Each hall is fronted by a massive pylon (ceremonial gateway), which originally

TUTANKHAMUN'S RESTORATION OF THE TEMPLES

As part of his promotion of the Aten to the status of Egypt's supreme deity, the pharaoh Akhenaten (ruled ca. 1353–1336BCE) closed down all the temples of Egypt's traditional gods. By the time his son Tutankhamun (ruled ca.1332–1322BCE) came to the throne, the temples had been abandoned for almost 20 years. However, the young king initiated a programme to restore the temples, whose state is described on the so-called "Restoration Stela": "Now his majesty appeared as king at a time when the temples of the gods and goddesses from the Delta to Aswan had fallen into ruins. Their shrines had collapsed and were overgrown with weeds until it seemed as if they had never existed. The land had been struck by catastrophe and the gods had turned their backs on Egypt. If anyone prayed to the gods they never came. Hearts were weakened in bodies, for what had been had been destroyed."

A detail of painted reliefs on the exterior of the Karnak barque shrine built by Alexander the Great's half-brother and successor Philip Arrhidaeus (reigned 323–317BCE). The barque contained the cult image of Amun from the temple's inner sanctuary. The sacred statue of the god is veiled from view within the central canopy.

marked the entrance to the temple and supported tall flagpoles which marked the site of the temple for miles around. In front of each pylon the gilded pyramidal tips of a pair of obelisks (tapered square columns) caught the first rays of the morning sun and, it was believed, transmitted their life-giving powers down into the temple.

Ten pylons were built in all, each designed to form a more splendid frontage to the temple than the last and each adorned with royal statues and enormous reliefs of the king smiting enemies with the gods looking on. From the final, outermost pylon, completed in Greco-Roman times, a processional avenue of ram-headed sphinxes once led to a harbour. Another avenue of sphinxes led southward to the temple of Mut and a third much longer avenue led to the temple of Amun more than a mile (1.6km) to the south at Luxor, magnificently rebuilt by Amenhotep III (ruled ca. 1390–1353BCE).

Egyptian temples were therefore very much "works in progress", frequently rebuilt, altered, expanded or repaired by successive monarchs. The gods had to be securely housed within their temples for Egypt to function effectively and to prevent chaos taking over, and restoration was essential following neglect during times of unrest or political turmoil, such as the tumultuous reign of Akhenaten (see box opposite). Egyptian culture was extraordinarily conservative and temple architecture changed relatively little over the millennia. So although some of the most intact temples – at

A pair of columns carved in the form of papyrus plants at the temple of Ramses III (ruled ca. 1187–1156BCE) at Medinet Habu. The best preserved of all the royal funerary temples of Western Thebes, it was also one of the largest, with a great entrance pylon 68 metres (267 feet) wide. The hieroglyphs on lower parts of the temple were deeply carved as a precaution against later erasure.

Dendera, Edfu, Esna and Philae – were built or rebuilt during the Greco-Roman era, they give a very good idea of what the temples they replaced looked like.

Temples were also erected on Egypt's margins to offer divine protection to those travelling long distances. Amenhotep III's first temple was built in honour of Nekhbet at the entrance to the mines of the Eastern Desert at el-Kab. Further afield, at Serabit el-Khadim in Sinai, there was a temple to Hathor, who as patron deity of the region was known as "Lady of the Turquoise", the mineral which was mined there.

In addition to the numerous temples serving Egypt's many deities, there were also funerary temples, known as "Mansions of Millions of Years", which were built to house the deified souls of deceased kings and to serve as the centre of their worship. Temples of the gods were generally built on the east side of the river, but funerary temples were built on the west bank, the land of the dead. They had their origins in funerary chapels attached to royal tombs, but they were eventually built as entirely separate structures when the tombs came to be built deep inside rocky valleys to deter robbers. The kings buried in the Valley of the Kings in Western Thebes built their funerary temples some distance away, nearer the river. The largest and most impressive of these ostentatious structures was built by Amenhotep III, but few traces of this survive (see box below). Among the most impressive extant remains are the temples of Hatshepsut, Ramses II (the Ramesseum) and the temple of Ramses III at Medinet Habu.

Egyptian temples could survive just about anything except the loss of the religion that underpinned them. This effectively happened in the fourth century CE, when the Roman Empire officially embraced Christianity and, in 392CE, closed all non-Christian places of worship. The good state of preservation of Philae and other temples owes much to their subsequent conversion into churches, though Philae itself continued to function as a temple of Isis for over a century and a half, a last outpost of a dying culture. But to some it seemed that the old gods and goddesses did not go quietly – Coptic texts record the early Church's struggle with pagan "demons" who, it was said, noisily haunted abandoned temples and terrified all who encountered them.

THE TEMPLE THAT DISAPPEARED

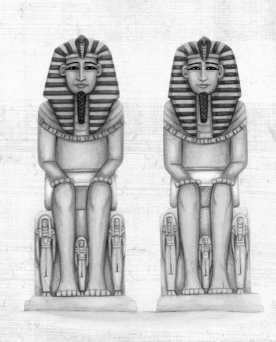

Now standing alone on the west bank of the Nile at Luxor, the two gigantic eroded statues known as the "Colossi of Memnon" once flanked the entrance to Egypt's biggest and most magnificent funerary temple. Built by Amenhotep III, of whom the colossi are portraits, it is described on a stela found at the site: "A monument for eternity everlasting, of fine sandstone worked with gold throughout. Its pavements are pure silver, all its doors fine gold. It is very great and wide and decorated with enduring images. It is adorned with this [stela] and my statues, made of granite, gritstone and every costly stone." Much of the temple's masonry was used by Ramses II and Ramses III for their own funerary temples. Such plundering, together with ancient earthquakes, mean that the two colossi are virtually all that remain of Amenhotep's vast structure.

SERVING THE GODS

Access to Egypt's temples was restricted to the priesthood, the "servants of the gods", and only on their authority were others permitted to enter the temple precincts. Only the king, who was regarded as Egypt's supreme high priest and the intermediary between humankind and the gods, could enter the inner sanctuary of a temple to address the sacred image of the deity directly. Egypt had hundreds of temples, so in practice he delegated this authority to the high priest of each temple. This senior cleric, most often called the First Servant (or First Prophet) of the relevant god or goddess, headed a hierarchy of male and female clergy whose posts were sometimes hereditary. Directly below him was the Second Servant, who acted as his deputy, and

RITUAL PURITY

All those admitted into the sacred precincts of the temple had to be ritually pure, otherwise they might be forcibly ejected. This entailed bathing twice during the day and twice at night in the temple's sacred lake, an artificial pool. Even the king had to undergo ritual bathing, but within the privacy of a royal palace attached to the temple, where a shower-like arrangement doused the monarch in water from the lake. In wall scenes the gods themselves pour out the waters, represented by a stream of *ankh* signs around the king. On entering the temple the king donned pure linen robes before being further "purified with incense and cold water".

Religious purity also involved the chewing of natron salts to freshen the mouth and the removal of all body hair. For both men and women, this included shaving the head. The priestesses who took the roles of Isis and Nephthys in the annual Mysteries of Osiris at Abydos (see page 101) had to be "women pure of body and who have not given birth, with the hair of their bodies removed, and their heads adorned with wigs".

This scene accompanies Spell 126 from *The Book of the Dead* of Khonsumose, a 21st-Dynasty priest at Karnak, and shows the Four Baboons who sit in the celestial barque of the sun god Ra. Here, the baboons are crouched around the four sides of the Lake of Fire, whose torches blaze between them. The symbolism of the square lake recalls the sacred pools that formed part of the general temple complex.

below them came the Third Servant and the Fourth Servant. Then there were specialist clergy such as "lector priests", who read out the sacred texts; "hour priests", skilled astronomers who regulated the timing of rituals and festivals; and funerary priests such as the *sem*, who wore leopard skins. Minor members of temple staff included gardeners, cattle-keepers and butchers. The great majority of priests and priestesses belonged to the general category of "purifiers" (masculine *waab* or feminine *waabet*), part-time clergy divided into four groups known as phyles, with each phyle being on duty for a month at a time. The total priesthood could range from a

Part of the wall painting from the well-room in the tomb of Ramses IX (ruled ca. 1126–1108BCE) in the Valley of the Kings, Western Thebes, depicts an Iunmutef or *sem* priest wearing his characteristic leopard skin while making funerary offerings to the dead king in the chamber below.

handful of officiants at a small temple to the more than 81,000 clergy employed at Karnak in the reign of Ramses III.

Priests and priestesses directed all their efforts toward serving the spirit of the deity who dwelled within his or her statue in a shrine within the inner sanctuary, a small chamber in the darkest and most remote part of the temple. The divine spirit was encouraged to remain within the statue with a constant stream of offerings presented in daily rituals that took place at dawn, midday and in the evening. Ordinary people – what we would call a congregation – were excluded from these rituals. The dawn ceremony was the most important. Amid copious clouds of purifying incense, a solemn procession of clergy headed by the high priest approached the inner sanctuary. The high priest entered the sanctuary and declared: "It is the king who sends me to see the god." After breaking the clay seals on the bronze doors of the god's cedarwood shrine – which was generally in the form of a barque (see page 103) – to reveal the god's statue, he uttered a hymn to awaken the divine spirit within the statue. One such hymn, from the temple of Khnum at Esna, begins: "Awaken gently in peace, awaken gently in peace, Khnum the ancient, who emerged from Nun in peace, awaken in peace, great Khnum."

The high priest would then announce: "I have seen the god, and the Powerful One has seen me" (an inscription from Edfu), before kissing the ground before the statue. Next, he offered the deity a small figure of Maat and anointed the deity's brow with perfumed oil. Thus purified, the statue would be dressed in linen and adorned.

Finally, the high priest would present the first offerings of the day, stacked up in the Hall of Offerings before the sanctuary. The walls of these offering chambers portray the great variety of items once presented, including bread, meat, fowl, fruit, vegetables, honey, milk, wine, beer, pure water, perfumes, oils, incense, lamps, salt and natron, clothing, jewelry and all manner of regalia and amulets. All offerings were regarded as gifts from the gods in the first place, and returning them to the gods as offerings bound deities and humans together in an endless cycle of mutual gratitude. Once the deity was deemed to have enjoyed its fill of offerings, there followed a ritual called the "Reversion of Offerings", in which the priests took away all the food and drink for their own consumption. Statues of royalty and eminent officials were set up throughout the temple so that they too might partake of the offerings.

The great quantities of daily offerings were largely given by the general population in the form of taxation, but they also included generous donations from the king and gifts from Egypt's empire. Many offerings were grown in the temple's often vast estates and gardens. As well as many tons of foodstuffs, millions of flowers were

WOMEN PRIESTS

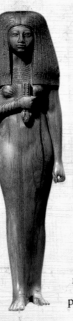

Outside the home, the most common career for Egyptian women was the priesthood. One of their most frequent roles was to entertain the deity as skilled singers, dancers or "chantresses". For example, Tuya, mother-in-law of Amenhotep III, was promoted to "chief of the entertainers" of both Amun and Min, as well as her role as a singer of Amun and Hathor. A surviving wooden figurine (right) shows her holding her sacred *menat* necklace which she would have shaken as a percussive accompaniment to temple ritual. Women some-times served as funerary priests and worked alongside men in royal jubilee ceremonies. They could even occupy the role of high priest, but this was rare. However, during the New Kingdom the office of "High Priestess of Amun" was bestowed on the king's daughter. Also known as "God's Wife of Amun", "God's Adorer" or "God's Hand", she fulfilled the role of Amun's wife at important rituals and at times enjoyed great political power, second only to the king.

needed both as offerings and for the manufacture of sacred perfume and incense – the fragrance of flowers was regarded as the very essence of the gods.

Libations (liquid offerings) were presented at the relatively simple midday ritual and a wide variety of lesser rituals went on throughout the temple during the day. At the evening ritual, performed before sunset, the high priest recited protective words and declared that "no male or female enemy shall enter this shrine". He then sealed the doors of the sacred shrine and withdrew, brushing away his footprints as he did so, until the following morning, when the cycle would begin all over again.

Just as the gods in their heavenly realm were gratefully worshipped by the living, so too were all those who had died and continued to live with Osiris in his underworld kingdom. The dead were venerated collectively as "the ancestors" and in the Ptolemaic *Book of Traversing Eternity* they are invited to take part in earthly festivals. Deceased relatives were honoured at small shrines within the home and were regarded as ever present and essential to the family's continuity and fertility.

Special honours were naturally accorded to dead kings in keeping with their status on earth, and they were worshipped at their funerary temples, each with its own priesthood (see pages 90–91). Individual rulers were often remembered and venerated for centuries after their deaths. Rituals were also performed to invoke the spirits of eminent commoners, most notably Imhotep, the royal architect of Egypt's first pyramid, the Step Pyramid, and Amenhotep son of Hapu, a high official under Amenhotep III. Both were widely worshipped for many centuries after their deaths and were regarded as the children of Thoth and Seshat, the god and goddess connected with writing and wisdom.

The dead were honoured at domestic shrines in the form of "ancestor busts", small stone stelae depicting the deceased as a blessed *akh iker en Ra* ("living spirit of Ra"). This bust is of Mutemonet, the mother of Amenmose, one of the scribes of Ramses II (ruled ca.1279–1213BCE).

ROYAL RITUALS

Scenes covering the surface of every temple in Egypt portray the king performing rituals before the gods. In practice these rites were usually carried out by his high priests, but there is a detailed description of King Piye (ruled ca. 747–716BCE) leading the rites of the sun god at Heliopolis: "The king is alone. He breaks the seals on the door bolts, and opens wide the doors to see his father Ra in the holy house of the Benben. He adores the morning barque of Ra and the evening barque of Atum. He closes the doors, applies the clay afresh and seals it with the royal seal."

The most common royal rituals involved the presentation of offerings. The chief royal offering was a figure of the goddess Maat, representing the divine order which the king upheld on earth. In return, the gods helped him in his task and bestowed life upon him in the form of *ankh* signs. The king reciprocated by making further offerings of food or drink. He is also shown holding out incense burners and perfumed ointment, with which he anoints the statue of the deity in its shrine.

The king generally stands to undertake his ritual duties, but he is also shown kneeling and even stretching out in a submissive pose before the gods. Only occasionally is he shown exerting himself physically. As part of the royal jubilee (*sed*) festivals held to mark the 30th anniversary of his accession, the king could be portrayed running to prove his fitness to rule (below), and straining to lift a great pillar (*djed*) representing stability. In scenes at his funerary temple at Medinet Habu, Ramses III can be seen undertaking strenuous manual work in the afterlife, scenes generally portrayed in private funerary texts rather than on royal monuments.

As high priest, the king was expected to provide music and dance for the deities, especially Hathor. In an inscription in his Theban tomb, King Inyotef II (ruled ca. 2065–2016BCE) declares: "I am he who makes the singer waken and make music for Hathor." In later times the king himself is described as the goddess's music-maker. Scenes of the Ptolemaic kings offering wine to Hathor at Dendera are accompanied by texts describing how the king, attired like a priest or priestess of Hathor with her sacred regalia of *menat* necklace and sistrum rattle, makes offerings while performing ritual dances to entertain her (see page 83).

THE DAILY OFFERING

A papyrus known as *The Admonitions of Ipuwer* belongs to a genre of Egyptian wisdom literature that centred around the opposition of order and disorder. It was written toward the end of the Middle Kingdom and describes a country beset with civil unrest with its ancient institutions in turmoil, where "foreigners have become [native] people everywhere" – shortly afterward, most of the country was occupied by a dynasty of Asiatic settlers. The text wistfully looks back to times of order, represented by the regular cycle of daily offerings to the gods:

"Remember the shrine,
 censing with incense,
 pouring sacred water from the libation
  vessel at dawn.
 Remember the offerings of fattened geese,
 the laying out of offerings to the gods.
 Remember chewing natron,
 with white bread prepared that day,
 remember setting up the flagstaffs,
 carving offering stones,
 the priest purifying the shrines
 and the inside plastered white like milk,
 sweetening the sanctuary,
 setting out the bread offerings."

DAYS OF FESTIVAL

The statues of the gods did not remain static within their temple sanctuaries, because the Egyptian sacred calendar included numerous public festivals at which they were transported in great processions by land and river on visits to each other's temples. Although the statues remained hidden from view inside their elaborate shrines, people were believed to benefit from the divine presence of the deity as it passed among them on the shoulders of the clergy. The processions would be accompanied by musicians and dancers, and entire local populations would turn out to join in the revelry and enjoy the huge quantities of food and drink that were freely avail-

THE FESTIVAL YEAR

The Egyptian year was punctuated by a series of annual festivals, beginning with New Year's Day at the start of Akhet, the season of the Nile flood. Some of the most important celebrations were as follows:

First Month of Akhet (Inundation): New Year's Day (July 19th); Wag Festival of Osiris at Abydos (see page 135); Festival of the Great Departure of Osiris; Festival of Thoth at Hermopolis; Hathor's Festival of Drunkenness at Dendera.

Second Month of Akhet: Festival of Opet at Luxor.

Fourth Month of Akhet: Festival of Hathor at Dendera; Festival of Sokar, god of cemeteries (day 26); Festival of Osiris at Abydos (possibly the same as the Mysteries of Abydos; see main text).

First Month of Peret (Spring Planting): Festival of Nehebkau, a snake god of the underworld and fertility (day 1); Festival of the Installation of the Sacred Falcon at Edfu (days 1–5).

Second Month of Peret: Festival of the Victory at Edfu (days 21–25, ca. January 9th–13th).

First Month of Shemu (Summer/Harvest): Festival of Min at Karnak.

Second Month of Shemu: Beautiful Festival of the Valley at Thebes.

Third Month of Shemu: Festival of the Joyous Union at Edfu (15 days from new moon to full moon).

Five Intercalary Days (between Fourth Month of Shemu and New Year): Birthdays of Osiris, Isis, Horus, Seth and Nephthys.

In this fragment of a limestone relief from a 19th-Dynasty tomb at Sakkara (ca. 1250BCE), women play tambourines and dance energetically, their hair swinging as they move, while two young girls dance and play clapsticks at the approach of a festival procession (right) led by a baton-carrying official who is being followed by male officials and scribes, their arms raised as a mark of rejoicing.

able during these public holidays – which were often the only times that most people ate meat. Such festivals were celebrated throughout the year for a variety of mythological, political or agricultural reasons, and their timings were carefully determined by the temple astronomers known as "hour priests".

Osiris in particular was honoured with great ceremonies during the year. During the annual Mysteries of Osiris held at his main religious centre of Abydos, the god's statue was taken in its barque from the temple to the traditional site of his tomb in the nearby desert. After a ritual reenactment of the conflict with Seth and the triumph of Osiris's followers, the god returned to his temple. One report of the occasion remarked that all the onlookers "rejoiced when they saw the beauty of the barque bringing Osiris, Foremost of the Westerners, Lord of Abydos, back to his palace."

Horus was also honoured in a series of festivals at Edfu. Surviving calendars at the temple list over 40 such events lasting from one day to two weeks, including the Installation of the Sacred Falcon, the Festival of the Victory (of Horus over Seth) and

A bronze sistrum (plural sistra), or sacred rattle, of the Greco-Roman period. It was played mainly by women and was closely linked with the worship of Hathor, whose head appears on the handle. Kings also wielded the sistrum when worshipping the goddess.

the Festival of the Joyous Union, when the statue of the goddess Hathor travelled south from her temple at Dendera to spend two weeks as the "guest" of Horus at Edfu. Hathor's 180km (112-mile) voyage to Edfu took two weeks because her glittering barque made several stops en route, including a visit to the goddess Mut at Karnak. As Hathor's barque sailed by, the riverbanks were filled with cheering people and it was claimed that even "the crocodiles became so calm that they did not rise up to attack".

One inscription vividly describes the festivities that accompanied Hathor's sojourn in Edfu: "There is every kind of bread, as many loaves as grains of sand. Oxen are as numerous as locusts, the smell of roast meat reaches to the skies. Wine flows freely through the town like the Nile flood bursting from its cavern. The myrrh and incense on the burners can be smelled a mile away and the whole city is strewn with faience, glittering with natron and bedecked with fresh flowers. ... Joy is all around and festivity is in every place. No sleep is to be had until dawn!"

At Dendera, Hathor was honoured at her own Festival of Hathor, during which her statue was taken out of her temple and presented to the people to celebrate a successful harvest. Music, dancing and drinking were a central feature of the proceedings. There were similarly exuberant annual festivals at many other places throughout Egypt, including el-Kab, Gebel Silsilah, Sakkara and Bubastis (see page 74).

Some of the most important festivals took place at Thebes, Egypt's religious capital. At the annual Beautiful Festival of the Valley, the statues of Amun, Mut and Khonsu crossed the river from Karnak to visit the royal funerary temples on the west bank. The processions would be accompanied by great crowds who would mark the occasion with a visit to the tombs of their loved ones. Other public ceremonies at Thebes involved the king and aimed to replenish his powers to commune with the gods. The greatest such ceremony was the annual Opet festival, at which the sacred statue of Amun was carried in its shrine from Karnak to Luxor, both by land and also in a great procession by river. At Luxor temple the statue was greeted by the king in a ritual hidden from public view. The walls of the temple illustrate events accompanying these royal rites, with priestesses shaking sistra alongside temple musicians and dancers whose ecstatic gyrations were emulated by the people when their reinvigorated monarch emerged, god-like, from the temple before them.

Other royal ceremonies might take place at least partly in public. These included the coronation, which featured great ritual processions; the royal jubilee, or *sed* (see page 97); temple foundation rites (see page 87) and the Festival of the Followers of Horus, a biennial ceremony celebrating the pharaoh's kinship with the gods.

THE SACRED BARQUES

The sacred regalia involved in rituals were made of the most expensive and exotic materials as a demonstration of each monarch's piety. This was especially true of the boat-shaped shrines in which the gods were housed in their temples and carried in processions. On the instructions of Sesostris III (ruled ca. 1836–1818BCE) "an everlasting great barque" of "gold, silver, lapis lazuli, bronze and cedar" was made for the statue of Osiris at Abydos. On finding a barque of Osiris to be made of native acacia, the 26th-Dynasty priest Peftuaneith ordered a replacement of cedar. The use of this prestigious and costly foreign wood was in part a political statement about a deity's imperial dominion. Amen-

hotep III commissioned a barque for Amun at Karnak "of new cedarwood cut on my orders in the Lebanon and dragged from the mountains by the chiefs of all foreign lands".

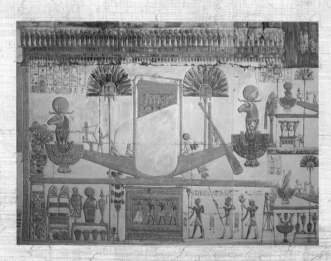

THE WORDS OF THOTH

Almost every available surface of every sacred building, whether tomb or temple, was covered in inscriptions in the Egyptian pictorial script, called "hieroglyphs" after the Greek for "sacred carving". The Egyptians themselves referred to their script as the "Words of Thoth", the ibis-headed god of writing who could also be represented as a baboon. Thoth, or Djehuty, was a child of the sun god Ra, who appointed him as his deputy to keep earthly affairs in order. According to myth, Ra allowed Thoth to give humans the knowledge of hieroglyphs, which was an essential tool for organizing and administering the country.

Historically, hieroglyphs are the earliest known form of writing, with recent discoveries dating as far back as ca. 3250BCE, before the first recorded dynasty of pharaohs. The script first developed as a way of recording produce, and as a tool of bureaucracy it rapidly became the means by which the Egyptian state took shape, with scribes working for the king to collect taxes and organize vast workforces.

It has been estimated that throughout ancient Egyptian history less than one per, cent of the population was literate. Scribes, or "followers of Thoth", were an elite and learned group, greatly praised in literature and described as "a noble profession". They were exhorted to "love writing, shun dancing, cease hunting, befriend the scroll and palette – they bring more joy than wine!" Senior officials and courtiers often had themselves portrayed as scribes to show that they were educated men. Horemheb, a senior military commander

A sculpture of Thoth as a baboon – a form derived from the way in which baboons greet the dawn (Thoth was the child of the sun god). The "Scribe of the Ennead", Thoth was the divine record keeper, preserving the wisdom of the ages. When the dead faced judgment before Osiris, Thoth recorded the verdict (see pages 124–125). Reign of Amenhotep III (ca. 1390–1353BCE).

Part of *The Book of Amduat* from the time of Tuthmosis III (ruled ca. 1479–1425BCE). The text is rendered in "cursive hieroglyphs", a simplified form of hieroglyphic script used for funerary writings, and red ink has been employed to highlight important sections.

under Tutankhamun who later became king (ruled ca. 1323–1295BCE), had himself portrayed in this way with an accompanying prayer to "Thoth, Lord of Writing". Prayers in *The Book of the Dead* identify the deceased as a divine scribe, the secretary of Ra: "Bring me a water pot and palette from the writing kit of Thoth, and all the mysteries which are in them. See – I am a scribe! Bring me the decomposition of Osiris, that I may write with it to copy down what the great good one says each day. I do right and run errands for Ra each day". Even the king is referred to in similar terms as the scribe of Ra, "opening his boxes, unsealing his documents, sealing his dispatches" (*Pyramid Texts*).

The Egyptians were great respecters of learning and there is a whole body of literature known as "wisdom texts" containing maxims advising how to live a good life and stressing the value of education. One such work, *The Instructions of Merikare*, claiming to be the words of King Merikare (ruled ca. 2015–2000BCE), exhorts: "Copy your ancestors. Their words endure in books. Open them! Read them! Copy their knowledge. He who is taught will become skilled." Scribes prayed to Thoth to give them wisdom: "O Thoth, come to me, Great Ibis, give me skill in your calling. It is better than anything else, it makes men great, and … fit to hold office." Both the god and his human counterparts are generally shown holding the tools of their trade: a reed pen, an ink palette and a water pot, which also represents the word *sesh*, meaning both "to write" and "scribe". The vast majority of scribes were male, but there are occasional images of women reading and some women held posts that would have required them to be literate, such as overseer, steward, doctor, vizier – and king.

Sacred texts such as those in the temple library at Edfu (see box opposite) were referred to collectively as "Books of Thoth". Ancient religious texts, as well as works of history, mathematics, medicine, geography, astrology and law were stored in temple libraries like those at the Ramesseum, Edfu, Dendera and Thoth's own cult centre of Hermopolis. There also seem to have been libraries in some of the royal palaces. Amenhotep III's palace at Malkata in Western Thebes incorporated a *per medjat* ("house of books") that included many works of a horticultural nature.

The inscriptions and accompanying images which cover Egypt's temples and tombs are arranged in ordered lines to give an overall feeling of balance. The small figures of humans, animals, birds and other symbols which populate hieroglyphic script were believed to infuse the scenes they accompanied with divine power, and rituals to "activate" the hieroglyphs were believed literally to bring these scenes to life. However, some signs were considered so potent that they were inscribed in two halves to diminish their power and prevent them from causing havoc when magically activated.

Despite their often complex meaning, in which a single symbol often represents an entire body of obscure mythology, the simple outlines and aesthetic appearance of hieroglyphs explains their use as both a decorative and functional device. They appear on all types of building, from monumental stone structures to simple mudbrick houses. The use of certain symbols in the home – including the home of the king – was especially important in areas associated with sleeping, where people were at their most vulnerable. The signs *ankh* ("life") and *sa* ("protection") were found in areas

THE HOUSE OF LIFE

The House of Life was one of the most important parts of each temple. It contained all forms of written texts, from sacred liturgy to ancient records, and it was also the place where scribes were educated in the art of writing. The meteoric rise of the 18th-Dynasty official Amenhotep son of Hapu began when he was sent to his local temple school in Athribis to be introduced to "the words of Thoth" and "the god's books" (the temple library). It was here, he says, that "I penetrated their secrets, and learnt all their mysteries". The *Building Texts* inscribed at Edfu refer to the temple's hieroglyphic inscriptions as being "beautifully inscribed by leading craftsmen in the House of Life, with all decoration being carried out according to the ancient records".

The House of Life at Edfu incorporated a well-preserved library called the "Library of Horus". None of the scrolls themselves have survived, but the niches in which they were once kept are inscribed with their titles. These reveal a fascinating mix of practical and esoteric works. In the former category are books such as *The Book of Temple Regulations* and *The Book of the Rota of Temple Guards*. A priest learning the sacred routines of the temple might also have consulted a manual entitled *The Book for Knowing the Secrets of the Laboratory, for Knowing the Details of the Gods' Offerings, the Lists of the Secret Forms of the God and Lists of the Deities which Live in this Temple and Never Leave this Place*. An astronomical manual, *Information about the Appearance of the Two Stars* [sun and moon] *and Periodical Return of Other Stars*, would have been referred to by the temple's "hour priests" to determine the timing of important festivals. The correct performance of such events would have been set out in books with titles such as *All Rituals Concerning the God Leaving his Temple in Procession on Festival Days* and *The Book for Sending Off the King in Procession*.

Many works were devoted to esoteric and magical rites aimed at warding off malign forces. These included *The Book for Performing Protection Rituals for the City, the Houses, the White Crown and the Year* and the *Books and Great Leather Rolls for Bringing About the Overthrow of the Evil One, Repelling Seth, Blessing the Hour and Preserving the Processional Boat* (see also page 110).

associated with childbirth, both on the walls and on items of furniture.

The majority of hieroglyphic inscriptions are simply endless repetitions of the names and titles of the kings and gods. But these are surrounded by protective symbols, because names were considered of tremendous importance and as vital to existence as the soul (*ka*). The loss of one's name meant permanent obliteration from history, and in order to prevent this, names were sometimes carved so deeply it is possible to place an outstretched hand inside each hieroglyph, as is the case of

ROYAL NAMES

Royal names were first written inside a protective rectangular fortress wall known as a *serekh*, which later developed into the more familiar oval-shaped cartouche. Every king had five names, but cartouches enclosed only the two most important, the "prenomen" and "nomen". The prenomen, or "King of Upper and Lower Egypt name", was assumed at the coronation and is so called because it is preceded by the phrase "King of Upper and Lower Egypt", written with the hieroglyphs of a sedge plant (Upper Egypt) and bee (Lower Egypt) (see page 37). The nomen, or "Son of Ra name", given at birth, is preceded by the phrase "Son of Ra" (*sa Ra*), written with the goose (*sa*) and sun (*ra*) signs. Amenhotep III, for example, is known today by his nomen,

which means "Amun is content [*hotep*]", but in his own time he was referred to in diplomatic correspondence only by his prenomen, Nebmaatra ("Ra, lord [*neb*] of truth [*maat*]"). The famous nomen of his grandson, Tutankhamun, means "Living [*ankh*] image [*tut*] of Amun".

The power of words was also harnessed in the form of the rebus, or visual pun. A sculpture of Ramses II portrays him crowned with the sun (*ra*) as a child (*mes*) holding the sedge (*su*) of Lower Egypt. The whole image thus spells out his name: *ra-mes-su*.

Royal names and titles were almost always followed by epithets such as "life, prosperity, health" and "given life forever". In such phrases the "key of life" (*ankh*) sign features prominently.

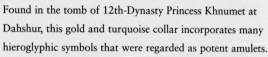

Found in the tomb of 12th-Dynasty Princess Khnumet at Dahshur, this gold and turquoise collar incorporates many hieroglyphic symbols that were regarded as potent amulets. They include the *tyet* knot representing the powers of Isis, the *djed* pillar of Osiris ("stability"), and the *ankh* sign (meaning "life"). Such amulets were worn as pendants, rings or pectorals by the living and the dead.

Ramses III's name and titles at his funerary temple (see illustration on page 90).

The written word was regarded as highly potent and the small number of individuals who could read and write were deemed to possess special powers via their privileged knowledge. Lector priests, who read out ritual texts during temple ceremonies, were often regarded as magicians, since it was they who spoke the magical "words of power" contained in the ancient scrolls.

The mystique surrounding the power of writing led to the development of myths about the existence of a magic book written by the god Thoth. It was believed to be hidden in an ancient tomb at Sakkara, northern Egypt, and was reputed to contain so much magic that its owner would be able to charm the entire universe and see the gods. By Greco-Roman times it was said that the entire knowledge of Egypt was contained in 42 books by Thoth, whom the Greeks identified with Hermes. So began the mystical tradition of "Thrice-Great Hermes" (Hermes Trismegistus) and his book of magical secrets, *The Hermetica*, whose fabled existence continues to intrigue the world.

As early as the Old Kingdom, scribes developed a simplified version of hieroglyphs known as hieratic (from Greek *hieratika*, meaning "sacred"), for day to day writing on papyrus or leather. By the Ptolemaic Period this had largely been superseded by an even more simplified form called "demotic" ("popular"). In Christian times the Egyptians adopted an alphabet known as Coptic that used Greek letters together with a few signs from demotic. However, full hieroglyphs remained the norm for monumental inscriptions of a religious nature, and they remained in constant use for almost 4,000 years until the end of the fourth century CE.

THE POWER OF MAGIC

In ancient Egypt there was no distinction between religion and magic. The Egyptians believed it was possible to alter their world by directing unseen forces, and sought to invoke and appease the spirits of gods and the dead to act on behalf of the living. The priesthood of state-organized temple religion employed magical rituals daily, as can be seen from books in the library of Edfu temple, which bore titles such as *The Book of Protecting the King in his Palace*, *The Book for Appeasing Sekhmet*, *Spells for Redirecting the Evil Eye*, *The Book of the Capture of the Enemy* and *The Book of Overthrowing Apophis* (see page 107). The rituals referred to in these texts were accompanied by the destruction of wax or clay images of anything which threatened the divine order or *maat*, from enemies of the state to the enemies of the sun god.

Those who uttered the sacred words at these magical rituals, the lector priests, are frequently referred to as magicians. In the Westcar Papyrus, the "chief lector priest and scribe of books" Djadjaemankh performs miraculous acts for King Snofru, while his son and successor, Khufu, calls upon the skills of Djedi, a 110-year-old man who "can join a severed head back on to its body, can make a lion walk on a lead behind him and knows the number of secret chambers in the sanctuary of Thoth". Numerous stories grew up around the magical abilities of Setna Khaemwese, a fictional character based on a son of Ramses II, Prince Khaemwaset, who had been high priest of Ptah at Memphis

A clay figurine of ca. 250CE of a kneeling woman pierced with nails and with her hands tied behind her back. However, the nails were intended not to cause physical harm but the pangs of love – the figurine was discovered inside a pot with a love charm, written in Greek on a lead tablet, that invoked the aid of Thoth, Anubis, the Roman demi-god Antinous and other magical beings.

and was described as "a very wise scribe and magician who spent all his time studying ancient books and monuments". In the first collection of tales, Setna Khaemwese searches for the magic book written by Thoth. It turns out to be in the possession of a dead magician called Naneferkaptah, and the two engage in a battle of magical skills. In another set of stories, Setna is taken down into the underworld by his son Siosire to compare the afterlife of the blessed with that of the damned.

Most Egyptians had no access to the state-sponsored magic performed in the temples, but practised their own smaller-scale rituals in their homes. Like the temple rites, domestic magic often involved the participation of both deities and the spirits of the ancestors. Magical rituals accompanied key rites of passage from birth to death. Childbirth in particular was accompanied by numerous protective spells and magical

DREAMS

The Egyptians believed in the power of dreams. Tuthmosis IV is said to have dreamed that he would gain the throne if he restored the Sphinx. He did so and later became king. Dreams were used to treat illness. Patients would sleep in the precincts of a temple; in the morning a priest interpreted their dreams with the aid of "dream books", such as the one shown here, of which this is an extract:

"If someone dreams of making love:
  bad. It means mourning.
If someone dreams of feeding cattle:
  bad. It means wandering the earth.
If someone dreams of falling into the river:
  good. It means purification from all evil."

procedures, as women appealed to Bes, Taweret and Hathor to protect both mother and child from evil spirits and to ease the birth (see page 73). According to the Ebers Medical Papyrus, a newborn baby would live if it cried "*ni*", whereas a cry of "*ba*" meant it would die. As the child grew up it would be protected by amulets and spells to ward off illness. One spell to cure fever asks: "Are you hot in the nest? Let there be brought a carnelian seal with a crocodile and hand to drive off this demon. The seal of the crocodile and hand to be made into an amulet and placed at the neck of the child." Amulets have been found that exactly match this description, being engraved with images of the protective crocodile and the magician's outstretched hand.

Egyptian medicine was therefore a combination of the practical and magical, with physical medical intervention complemented by the use of incantations and amulets.

THE SECRET NAME OF RA

Names had a magical potency and it was believed that knowing a person's name gave one great power over them. A famous spell to neutralize poison says that "Isis was more clever than a million gods and knew everything in heaven and on earth" except for Ra's secret name. If Isis could learn the secret name of Egypt's supreme deity her power over him would be limitless. Another means of gaining power over someone was to obtain part of their physical being. Since Ra was an elderly god who dribbled as he slept, Isis mixed his saliva with earth to make a poisonous snake. This later bit Ra, who fell into a raging fever and screamed in agony. But none of the gods could help and the sun's powers began to dwindle. Then Isis claimed she could cure Ra if he told her his secret name. Despite his pain, Ra refused and tried to fool Isis with a long list of his other titles. But Isis did not relent and eventually Ra told her his name on the understanding that Isis swore never to reveal it. Nor is the name revealed in the story – only the goddess's cure, which involves wine or beer mixed with "herb of the scorpion".

An 18th-Dynasty white faience cosmetic pot in the form of the god Bes. A benign dwarf deity whose grotesque appearance was intended to ward off malign forces, Bes was particularly popular in the home. He was invoked in childbirth and his image was often painted on the walls to protect the inhabitants.

Medical practitioners were often priests of Sekhmet, who hoped that by devoting themselves to the goddess they could curb her ability to bring disease. One spell refers to the causes of sickness as "disease demons and malignant spirits, the messengers of Sekhmet", and the Ebers Medical Papyrus recommends calling upon the services of a "physician, Sekhmet priest or exorcist" to deal with medical problems. Similarly, devotees of the scorpion goddess Selket dealt with scorpion bites. Isis appears as protector of her son Horus in spells dealing with snake and scorpion bites as well as burns, as in this example: "Mix together the milk of a woman who has a son with gum and ram's hair. Apply it to the burn while saying: 'Your son Horus is burnt in the desert and needs water. But I have water in my mouth and the Nile between my thighs and I am here to extinguish the fire.'" The talents of Isis are expressed to the full in a spell to neutralize poison involving Ra's secret name (see box opposite). A bath in water from a temple's sacred lake was also believed to have a curative effect, as was a drink of water which had first been poured over a statue of a god or other revered figure.

Magic could also be used to cause harm. Wax or clay figurines were employed to direct such magic as precisely as possible, especially if it incorporated a piece of hair from the intended victim. Clay figures of enemies were smashed to annihilate those whom they represented, whereas wax images could be burnt, impaled with needles or bound with thread. The royal women who were put on trial for an assassination attempt on Ramses III are said to have made wax figurines of the palace guards in order to overwhelm them. Such figurines could be inscribed with curses or "execration texts" to make them even more effective.

THE JOURNEY
OF THE SOUL

Just as the living inhabited the earth and the gods dwelled in the heavens, the dead lived in Duat, the underworld, under the rule of Osiris. Only the gods and the dead could move among all three realms. The dead might roam the earth as spirits or join with the gods in the skies, while the gods were present on earth in their cult statues and also played a vital role in Duat. The dead faced the judgment of Osiris; those who passed this ordeal went on to an eternal blissful existence in a perfected underworld version of Egypt.

DEATH AND THE AFTERLIFE

Egyptians planned for their deaths for years in advance, so that they would have all the items necessary to secure their safe passage to "the west" – the afterlife. In an age when death could be sudden and few people lived past middle age, nothing was left to chance and all manner of elaborate preparations were made for the day when the soul would leave the earth and set off on its journey through Duat. Although they were naturally affected by the deaths of loved ones, death was regarded not as the end of existence but simply as the beginning of another stage.

The Egyptians regarded each individual as made up of a number of separate elements: the name; the body and the heart; the shadow or shade (*shuwt*); and the *ka* and *ba*. At death a person ceased to be confined to the physical body and could exist as an invisible spirit comprising the two separate entities of *ka* and *ba*. Often translated as "soul", the *ka* was a person's vital life force or energy, created with them at birth and remaining with them throughout their life on earth and beyond. The *ka* was sustained with food and drink and at night it generally resided within the corpse or "*ka* statue" (left).

The *ba*, or "spirit", constituted the essential personality of the deceased. Like the *ka*, it was sustained with food and drink offerings and had to return to the mummy at night, but unlike the earthbound *ka* it was highly mobile – it was the *ba* that made the perilous journey through the underworld. Depicted as a bird with the head of the deceased, it could flit among the worlds of gods, humans and the dead

This lifesize wooden sculpture stands 1.7m tall and represents the *ka* of King Awibra Hor of the 13th Dynasty (ruled ca. 1370BCE). The arms on his head, outstretched in a protective embrace, represent the hieroglyphic symbol for *ka*. Such images were provided as a home for the *ka* in case the deceased's mummy should be destroyed.

and could change shape at will in order to avert danger. When the *ba* had passed through the perils of the underworld it was able to reunite with the *ka* and transform the deceased into an *akh*, or transfigured spirit.

Both the *ba* and *ka* needed the shelter of the physical body. This led to the development of mummification as a means of retaining the lifelike appearance of the body – essential if it was to be recognized by its *ka* and *ba* (see box on page 119). Once the corpse had been mummified and finally laid in its coffin, the funeral could take place. *The Story of Sinuhe* describes the "mummy case of gold, its head of lapis lazuli" on a hearse drawn by oxen, with singers going on before and dancers performing at the tomb. The procession would be led by priests and accompanied by family, friends and servants carrying the deceased's funerary goods and personal belongings. The wealthy

WRITINGS FOR THE DEAD

Few Egyptians of means would risk being buried without a "guide book" to the perils of the afterlife. Inscribed inside nine pyramids around the end of the Old Kingdom, the 800 or so spells or utterances of the *Pyramid Texts* – the world's oldest group of religious texts – aim to protect the king on his journey to an afterlife among the gods. They were later adapted for non-royal use and inscribed on coffins (right). These *Coffin Texts* run to more than 1,000 spells or chapters and increasingly stress the underworld of Osiris as the destination of the dead. By the New Kingdom many of the *Coffin Texts* had been incorporated in a body of writings known as *The Book of the Dead*, with 200 or so chapters. Generally written on papyrus and placed in the coffin, it includes a chapter on the judgment before Osiris, a scene often illustrated (see pages 124–129).

A painted funeral scene detail (ca. 1350BCE) from the Theban tomb of vizier Ramose, showing a group of professional female mourners and their young apprentices hired to perform during Ramose's funerary rites. As mourners, they threw dust on their heads and pulled at their hair.

might also hire male and female professional mourners. On reaching its final resting place, the coffin was greeted by *muu* dancers, enigmatic male figures who performed a ritual dance representing the solemn moment when the dead crossed the threshold between the worlds of the living and the dead.

Next, the coffin was stood upright before the tomb. Supported by a masked priest representing Anubis, the god of embalming, it was purified with oils and incense. Then, as a lector priest read out incantations, the elaborate "Opening of the Mouth" ceremony was performed by the heir of the deceased or the *sem* priest, a funerary priest associated with Ptah. The deceased's mouth, eyes, ears and nose were symbolically reopened with ritual implements in a rite designed to reawaken all the senses and allow the deceased to absorb all the offerings that would be presented to them.

With the spirit reactivated and senses primed, the deceased was finally laid to rest in the tomb, surrounded by as many funerary goods as he or she could afford, from a few pottery vessels containing food and drink for the majority to the golden treasures of the wealthiest. Funerary goods included small figurines of the deceased called *shabti*s, who would perform work for the deceased in the afterlife.

For most people a grave was rarely more than a hollow in the sand. In contrast, the tombs of the wealthy were elaborate and beautifully decorated, often carved out of

Just as the spirit of a god inhabited its statue, the spirit of the deceased resided in its mummy, which was regarded as a sacred entity. The process of embalming was also sacred, since it was a reenactment of the mummification of Osiris (see page 60). Each stage of the complicated 70-day procedure was accompanied by ritual incantations to create the perfect and incorruptible vessel for the soul.

Mummification was carried out in the "place of embalming" or "house of purification" (*per wabet*), which had to be ritually pure and protected from malign forces so that no harm would befall the deceased as he or she lay vulnerable and inanimate on the embalming table within. The Egyptians were also well aware of more obvious threats to the corpse: a chapter of *The Book of the Dead* is called "Spell for repelling a beetle".

To prevent putrefaction the internal organs were removed and mummified separately. However, the heart was always left in the body, because the Egyptians believed it to be the seat of all emotion and wisdom and vital to the continued well-being of the dead. The body was then dried out for 40 days beneath natron salts before being washed and anointed with perfumed oils. The procedure was similar to that used on cult statues of deities and aimed to imbue the body with all the protective powers of the gods as well as "to unite the limbs, join the bones and assemble the flesh". The oils were also believed to repel harmful forces, and indeed they provided a protective coating against bacteria responsible for decomposition.

In order to pass into the afterlife the deceased had to be pure, clean, anointed and clothed in "fresh linen". Up to 375 square metres of material might be used to wrap the mummy. Protective amulets, including *wedjat* eyes of Horus, *djed* pillars of Osiris, and *tyet* knots of Isis, were placed among the layers of wrappings at selected points to offer maximum protection for those parts. The most important amulet was the scarab placed directly over the heart, the seat of the intellect. Then the mummy would be laid in its wooden coffin, which was painted with protective deities and texts, or gilded and inlaid if the owner could afford it. All was now ready for the rites to reactivate the *ka* of the deceased (see main text).

solid rock. The tomb was "a house of death which is for life" and it was here, in the associated funerary chapel or temple, that the deceased would be venerated by the living. The tomb was also the starting point for the long journey through the underworld and into the afterlife. Although the conventional term "underworld" suggests a place beneath the earth, Duat was often described as existing in the skies. Most sources agree that Duat was a place devoid of light. However, much of it was illuminated every night by the sun god as he passed through on his journey between the western and eastern horizons. To attain the blessed afterlife, the deceased had to traverse the same perilous places faced by the sun on his nightly voyage through the 12 hours of the night. Each hour was regarded as a separate region or cavern, with names such as "Deep Waters" and "City of Corpse-Counting". Each cavern had a gateway, guarded

CREATURES OF THE UNDERWORLD

Many of Egypt's great deities had a funerary aspect alongside their roles within their heavenly and earthly domains. However, certain divinities existed only within Duat. Many were judges of the dead (see pages 124–129), others were guardians of the under-world's gates and caverns. *The Book* of *Amduat* names the powerful deities who dwelled in the 12 regions of the underworld and helped Ra against his foes. They include "Splitter of the Skulls of Ra's Enemies", "Repeller of the Snake", "Slicer of Souls" and "Beheader of Rebels". *The Book of Gates* lists the serpents who guarded the gates of each region, including "Stinger", "Flame Face", and "Effluent One". The deceased had to know all their names to be allowed to pass. The underworld was also home to evil and terrifying forces that preyed on unsuspecting souls with nets and spears. Again, only by knowing the correct way to address such entities could the deceased render them harmless.

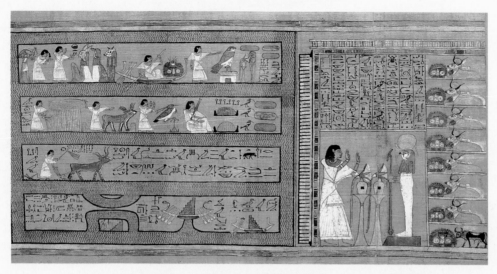

Part of the scribe Ani's *Book of the Dead* (ca. 1250BCE) illustrating Chapter 110 (left) in which he undertakes farming in the Fields of Reeds, harvesting crops and using oxen to tread the grain and plough the fields. He also worships the Falcon of the West, the Heron of Plenty and three gods of the Ennead. In Chapter 148 (right), Ani worships Ra, the Seven Celestial Cows and the Bull of Heaven.

by a different set of hour goddesses, demigods, demons or serpents. In order to pass through on their way to rebirth, it was essential that the spirits of the dead were able to utter these guardians' names to neutralize their power. After negotiating the final cavern, one final ordeal remained: judgment before Osiris (see pages 124–129).

On their hazardous and often terrifying journey through Duat, the deceased could take comfort from the presence of their divine protectors, chief among whom was the creator sun god, whose life-giving energy would sustain them eternally. But it was Osiris who ruled over the dead. As Khentamentiu ("First of the Westerners"), he was the first being to experience death and so enter the land of the dead, where he was the salvation of all who died and the one who gave eternal hope to the living. Osiris, with Isis and Horus, provided maximum protection for the dead. Isis, Nephthys, Neith and Selket were responsible for the safety of the deceased's viscera, together with four deities known as the Sons of Horus. Nut also played a key role in protecting the deceased, as did Hathor, who emerged from the Theban hills to receive the dead.

AN OFFERING FOR NEFERHOTEP

In a land famed for its grandiose funerary buildings, some of the most touching monuments are the simple stone stelae commemorating ordinary Egyptians. One was erected by the friend of a singer called Neferhotep, who appears to have had no family of his own and is portrayed endearingly as an extremely rotund character reaching out toward a well-stocked offering table. The moving dedication opens with a standard offering formula on behalf of the king and ends, unusually for Egyptian art, with the "signature" of the craftsman who made the stela.

"An offering which the king gives
to Osiris, Lord of Abydos,
and Horus, son of Isis,
that they may give offerings of bread, beer,
beef and fowl,
alabaster vessels and linen
and every good and pure thing
for the *ka* of the singer Neferhotep,
true of voice [without sin],
born of the housewife Henu.
His beloved friend, the brick-carrier Nebsumenu,
had this made for him.
Alas!
Be kind to him!
The draughtsman Sonebau, son of Rensoneb."

IN THE HALL OF JUDGMENT

After the journey through the underworld, the deceased had one more challenge to face before entering the afterlife: the judgment of Osiris. *The Book of Gates* locates the Hall of Osiris, where the dead were judged, beyond the fifth gate of the underworld. Here Osiris sat enthroned on a dais, like the pharaoh on earth, holding his regal crook and flail as symbols of his power. The god was often accompanied by his sisters, Isis and Nephthys, and sometimes by two identical figures of the goddess Maat to emphasize that this judgment chamber – also known as the Hall of Two Truths – was the seat of truth, justice and order. Osiris presided over a tribunal of 42 gods known as the Assessors, the judges of the dead, who had forbidding names such as "Shadow-Eater", "Flinty-Eyed" and "Beaky".

After being led into the hall by the god Anubis, the deceased stood in the presence of Osiris and the Assessors to utter the "Negative Confession" from *The Book of the Dead*. This involved reciting, one by one, a lengthy list of sins that the deceased denied having committed (see pages 127–129). The truth of the confession was confirmed by weighing the heart of the deceased against the feather of Maat on a pair of tall scales that stood in the centre of the great hall. One purpose of the scarab amulet placed over the heart during mummification (see page 119) was to ensure that it spoke the truth before Osiris. The amulet bore words from *The Book of the Dead*, beginning: "O heart which I had from my mother, do not stand against me, do not act as a witness against me, do not oppose me in the tribunal!"

As Anubis checked the scales and Thoth stood by to record the outcome, the dead person waited nervously for the verdict on his or her eternal soul. If the deceased had spoken the truth and had indeed led a life free of sin, the heart and the feather would be in perfect balance and the tribunal would declare the departed to be "true of voice". This moment is often depicted in *The Book of the Dead*, with the deceased, assured of a blissful immortality, shown with arms upraised in jubilation and relief.

Finally, the deceased was led by Horus to the throne of Osiris and exhorted to "throw away your mask and undo your wrappings!" He or she then entered the afterlife as a glowing, transfigured spirit (*akh*), standing before the sun god and basking in his power, having become an "able spirit of Ra", free of earthly impediments.

A very different fate awaited those who failed to pass the test of truth. Egyptians were warned that "wrongdoers shall not behold the face of god", and hearts heavy with sin that tipped the scales were instantly thrown to a monster called Ammut ("Devourer", see illustration on page 135), who crouched in wait by the scales. A composite creature with a crocodile's head, lion's body and hippopotamus's hind legs, Ammut would swallow the heart and in doing so consign the unfortunate sinner to eternal oblivion.

This vignette from *The Book of the Dead* shows the weighing of the heart of Turiu, a Theban priest of the 21st Dynasty. Anubis checks the scales of Maat (centre), which are in perfect equilibrium, while the deceased raises his arms in delight. Thoth looks on with his pen ready to record the verdict.

THE CONFESSION BEFORE OSIRIS

Chapter 125 of *The Book of the Dead* instructs the deceased on what to say "on arriving at the Hall of Two Truths" in the presence of Osiris. They had to recite the "Negative Confession" in order to demonstrate that they were completely free of sin ("true of voice") and thus entitled to enter the afterlife as a blessed spirit and "see the face of every god". The following is an extract:

"I have not committed crimes against people.

I have not mistreated cattle.

I have not sinned in the place of truth [temple or necropolis],

I have not known that which should not be known,

I have not done any harm,

I have not exacted more than was my due,

I have not committed blasphemy against the gods,

I have not robbed the poor,

I have not done what the gods hate,

I have not spoken ill of a servant to their master,

I have not caused pain,

I have not caused tears,

I have not killed or ordered anyone to kill,

I have not caused suffering,

I have not damaged the temple offerings,

I have not stolen bread from the gods,

I have not stolen bread from the dead,

I have not committed adultery nor defiled myself,

I have not falsified the measures,

I have not taken milk from children's mouths,

I have not kept cattle from their pastures,

I have not extinguished a necessary fire,

I have not neglected the time of meat offerings,

I have not held back the cattle of the gods,

I have not stopped a god in procession.

I am pure! I am pure! I am pure! I am pure!

I am pure as the great heron of Hnes [Herakleopolis Magna]!

No harm shall befall me

in this Hall of Two Truths,

for I know the names of all the gods within it,

all the followers of the great god [Osiris]:

O Wide-Strider of Heliopolis, I have not done evil;

O Flame-Embracer of Kheraha, I have not committed robbery;

O Beaky of Khmun, I am not guilty of greed;

O Shadow-Eater from the Cave, I am not guilty of stealing;

O Terrifying Face of Rostau, I am not guilty of murder; …

O Wrecker from Huy, I am not guilty of trespass;

O Bastet of the Shrine, I am not guilty of winking;

O Backward Face of the Pit, I am not guilty of homosexuality. …

Hail to you gods!

I know you and know your names,

I shall not fall down in fear of you,

You shall not accuse me of a crime!"

THE DEAD AND THE LIVING

In Egypt the dead were never felt to be very far away and they were regularly consulted by the living in a variety of ways. People would approach their own deceased relatives for aid and advice on domestic and personal matters as they no doubt did in life, and they could also call upon famous wise figures of the past, including monarchs such as Amenhotep I and officials such as Imhotep and Amenhotep son of Hapu, whose reputations for wisdom were so great they were deified after death. The living could address the deceased directly with prayers when visiting their tombs with offerings. The dead were regarded as possessors of magical power (*heka*), and their tombs

A LAMENT FOR ISENKHEBE

The Egyptians were greatly concerned with the well-being of children and amulets and spells were widely employed to protect babies and infants. However, death in childhood was very common and was regarded with particular sadness. At Sais in the Delta a mother and father erected an inscription in memory of their baby daughter Isenkhebe that speaks poignantly of their grief at the loss of one so young: "Although I am

only a child, harm befell me when I was only a child. I was driven from my childhood too early, turned away from my home when still young. The terrifying dark engulfed me while the breast still fed me. The demons here keep all away, but I am too young to be alone. I enjoyed seeing people and my heart loved joy. O Lord of Eternity to whom all people come, give me bread, milk, incense and water from your altar. I am a young girl without fault!"

An artwork based on a simple pottery offering bowl inscribed with a "letter" to a dead relative – one of only two dozen or so such bowls thus far discovered. The addressee is depicted in the centre of the bowl, which would have been filled with food offerings and left in the deceased's tomb.

were places of tremendous magical potency which could be harnessed for the benefit of the living. It was also possible to make contact with those in the afterlife through the skills of the local female seer, or *ta rekhet* ("woman who knows" or "wise woman") – women were believed to possess the intuitive powers necessary to communicate with unseen forces.

Requests for help could also take the form of letters to the dead written on papyrus (rolled or folded up), on linen or even on the bowls in which offerings were placed. The contents of such letters were often discussions of practical matters, such as disputed wills, or requests for the dead to intercede with the gods. After having a recurring dream suggesting that he was responsible for the death of the family servant, a Tenth-Dynasty priest called Seni left a letter at the tomb of his dead father Meru appealing for him to vouch for his innocence to the gods.

As those who had been given new life, the dead were approached for help in conceiving children, with such requests being written on fertility figurines. A Greek couple called Leon and Lysandra left a dedication to Amenhotep son of Hapu – some 1200 years after his death – thanking him for the birth of their child.

Many messages requested cures for illnesses. In the Tenth Dynasty a sick man called Merirtifi wrote a letter to his late wife Nebitef that opens in homely fashion: "How are you? Is the west taking care of you properly?" He goes on to ask her to "drive off this illness in my limbs." There are also touching letters that simply express an individual's grief and ask the deceased why they have gone away. One man tells his wife that after her death he had stood in the street and wept.

Part of *The Book of the Dead* of Queen Nodjmet ca. 1070BCE, with the deceased seated beside her husband Herihor before a well-stocked offering table in the presence of the gods and an officiating priest. Behind them, providing sustenance for the deceased, are the Bull of Heaven and four of the Celestial Cows.

These letters reveal that the blessed dead were not always benign. Some returned to harass those who had failed to honour their memory, perhaps by not making adequate offerings or giving them proper burial. These disgruntled *akh*s haunted cemeteries and could even possess people's bodies and cause illness. In the 12th Dynasty a woman called Dedi wrote to her dead husband: "Our servant Imiu is ill. Why don't you fight for her night and day with the man or woman who is doing her harm? If you don't help, the household will simply fall apart."

Worse than the troublesome *akh*s were the evil spirits (*mut*) of dead people whose lives had been unhappy or unfulfilled, or who had suffered violent or premature ends. Some had died a "second death" by failing the test of truth before Osiris (see pages 124–125) and were making one last attempt to traumatize the living before their souls were annihilated. These hostile spirits, referred to as "enemies from the west", roamed the land looking for a chance to attack the living. Their attacks generally came at night, when potential victims were sleeping and at their most vulnerable, and took the form of nightmares, sickness or even death. People defended themselves with various amulets and spells invoking individual deities to watch over the family during the night.

THE GHOST OF THE KING

A writing called *The Instruction of King Amenemhat* describes how, following his bloody assassination at the hands of his own bodyguards, the ghost of the Middle Kingdom pharaoh Amenemhat I (ruled ca. 1939–1909BCE) returned to tell his beloved son and successor Sesostris I to beware of traitors in his midst. This work survives in numerous fragmentary New Kingdom copies on papyrus, wooden tablets and shards of pottery.

"Listen to what I tell you", the ghost says, "so you may rule and govern well, and increase well-being!" He goes on to warn the young king against "nobodies, whose plots remain hidden", and advises him to "trust no-one, neither a brother nor a friend; have no intimates, they are worthless".

There follows an account in the king's own words of how he was murdered: "It happened after supper, when night had come, as I rested peacefully for an hour, weary on my bed. As my heart turned to sleep the weapons of my protection were turned against me. I awoke fighting to find the bodyguard attacking. If only I had been quick enough and seized my weapons I would have made the cowards retreat at once! But none are mighty in the night and none can stand alone without a helper close beside. And all this happened while I was without you, before the court knew I would hand everything over to you, before I had been able to sit with you and tell you of my plans. For I had not prepared for this, had not foreseen the treachery of servants!"

Finally, the royal ghost bids farewell: "Sesostris my son! I must leave you now and turn away. But you are always in my heart and my eyes will always see you! My child of a happy hour! I have established a beginning and wish to plan the future, giving you the contents of my heart. You are my likeness, and wear the white crown of your divine father. Everything is as it should be."

Before returning to the heavens to "board the barque of Ra", the dead pharaoh offers one last piece of advice: "Fight for all the wisdom the heart knows – for you will need it with you always."

A scene from the inside of the sarcophagus of 22nd-Dynasty priest Ankhefenkhonsu from Thebes, which shows the deceased presenting lavish offerings to Osiris. From letters to the dead and other inscriptions it appears that an *akh* could intercede directly with the gods.

Tomb inscriptions sometimes include curses in which the owner threatens to use his or her power as an *akh* to punish trespassers, as in this example from the tomb of an Old Kingdom lector priest called Ankhmahor at Sakkara: "I am an excellent lector priest, knowledgeable in secret spells and all magic. As for anyone who enters my tomb impure ... I shall seize him like a goose [choke him] and fill him with fear at the sight of ghosts upon earth, so that he might fear an excellent *akh*!"

It was the duty of the living to sustain the *ka*s of the deceased with adequate funerary offerings and prayers, "because they will starve without sustenance and perish". On a Middle Kingdom stela the royal seal bearer Nebankh is told by the singer Tjeniaa: "You are firm in your seat of eternity [tomb], your everlasting monument, which is filled with offerings and food and every good thing."

Royal tombs were generally hidden to protect their priceless contents and so dead kings were honoured at separate funerary temples (see pages 90–91). However, the tombs of the general populace were easily accessible, and families would make regular trips to them to present offerings to the deceased, often coinciding their outings with religious festivals. At the annual Beautiful Festival of the Valley at Thebes (see page 102), great crowds of revellers took the opportunity to visit the tombs of their loved ones and make offerings of food and flowers distributed by the Theban temples

and potent with divine essence. The annual Wag Festival of Osiris, held on a night in mid-August, was a kind of Egyptian Hallowe'en, when generous offerings were made to all those in the afterlife. The deceased were also encouraged to be present at public holy days for the benefit of the living. Paheri, a mayor of Nekhen (el-Kab) during the New Kingdom, declares in his tomb that he will attend all the festivals after his death, "clothed in the finest linens as worn by the gods, anointed with the purest oil".

The wealthy employed *ka* priests to provide them with a regular supply of offerings (*kaw*) after their deaths and recite all the necessary prayers. In this way the funerary cults of both kings and commoners could last for centuries. But even if their names were finally forgotten, the Egyptians believed that the offerings buried with the dead and depicted on their tomb walls would magically sustain them into eternity.

INTO THE UNKNOWN

Despite their general optimism about death, many Egyptians had doubts about what came after, especially in times of instability and insecurity. A body of "pessimistic literature" reflects such occasional scepticism. In one 11th-Dynasty song, the uncertainties of death encourage a carefree lifestyle: "What has become of [the dead]? … None return from there to describe it, / to tell us of their needs / and calm our hearts / until we go where they have gone! / So be happy! / Forget your troubles / and follow your heart as long as you live! /

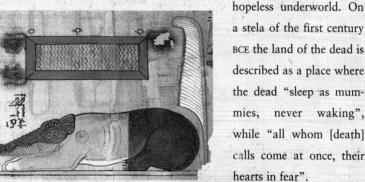

… For none who departs comes back!" These lyrics were circulated for centuries, but their over-hedonistic attitude was sometimes frowned upon. The Egyptian sceptical streak grew stronger under the rule of the Greeks and Romans, for whom death was a grim deity who led the deceased to a bleak and hopeless underworld. On a stela of the first century BCE the land of the dead is described as a place where the dead "sleep as mummies, never waking", while "all whom [death] calls come at once, their hearts in fear".

GLOSSARY

Cross-references to other terms in the glossary are in bold type.

akh The blessed transfigured spirit of a dead person, resulting from the merging of the *ka* and *ba*.

atef A plumed crown worn by the king on certain ritual occasions.

aten The disc or orb of the sun, the visible manifestation of the sun god. It was worshipped as a god in its own right (the Aten) in the reigns of Amenhotep III and, especially, his son Akhenaten.

ba The "spirit" of the deceased, constituting his or her essential personality.

Book of the Dead, The Funerary texts written on papyrus, made up of ca. 200 chapters or "spells" to ensure a proper burial and safe passage into the afterlife.

Coffin Texts Funerary texts painted or inscribed on coffins, made up of ca. 1,000 spells to ensure a proper burial and safe passage into the afterlife.

djed pillar A symbol of stability, usually said to represent the backbone of the god Osiris.

faience Glazed ceramic, usually bright blue in colour.

hieroglyphs The Egyptian writing system, whereby pictures or symbols represented sounds, concepts or things. They were mainly used for temple and tomb inscriptions; shorthand forms (hieratic and demotic) developed for use on papyrus or leather.

Intermediate Period A term given to each of the periods between the **Old Kingdom** and **Middle Kingdom**, the Middle Kingdom and **New Kingdom**, and the New Kingdom and **Late Period**. The three Intermediate Periods are characterized by relative political instability and national disunity.

ka A person's life-force or energy.

Late Period The last period in which Egypt was ruled by native kings (664–332BCE, interrupted by two periods of Persian rule, 525–405BCE and 343–332BCE).

ma'at "Truth", "order", a cosmic principle revered in the form of the goddess Ma'at (see page 19).

Middle Kingdom The second great flowering of Egyptian civilization, covering the 11th to 13th dynasties of pharaohs (ca. 2081–1630BCE).

mortuary temple or **funerary temple** A temple erected for the worship of a deceased and deified king.

natron A naturally occurring salt compound used in ritual purification and for drying a corpse during mummification.

New Kingdom The third and greatest flowering of Egyptian civilization, covering the 18th to 20th dynasties of pharaohs (ca. 1539–1075BCE).

Old Kingdom The first great flowering of Egyptian civilization, covering the 3rd to 6th dynasties of pharaohs (ca. 2625–2130BCE).

pharaoh A king of Egypt, a Greek term from the Egyptian *per-aa* ("great house"), which originally applied to the royal palace but from the **New Kingdom** was also used to refer to the king.

Ptolemaic Period Era of rule (310BCE–30BCE) by the Greek dynasty founded by Ptolemy I; it sometimes includes the reigns of Alexander the Great, Philip III and Alexander IV (332–310BCE).

Pyramid Texts Funerary texts painted and inscribed inside a number of **Old Kingdom** pyramids, made up of 800 spells to ensure the king's proper burial and safe passage into the afterlife.

Ramesside era The 19th and 20th dynasties, spanning the reigns of Ramses I to Ramses XI (ca. 1292–1075BCE).

stela A flat piece of stone or wood, bearing an inscription or a relief or both. Stelae were commonly set up to commemorate the dead.

FURTHER READING

BIBLIOGRAPHY

Andrews, C. *Amulets of Ancient Egypt*. London, BMP, 1994.

Baines, J. and J. Malek. *The Atlas of Ancient Egypt*. Oxford, Phaidon, 1980; New York, Facts on File, 1993.

Benard, E. and B. Moon, eds. *Goddesses Who Rule*. New York, Oxford University Press, 2000.

Faulkner, R.O., ed. C. Andrews. *The Ancient Egyptian Book of the Dead*. London, BMP, 1989; ed. C. Andrews et al. San Francisco, Chronicle Books, 1994.

Forman, W., and S. Quirke. *Hieroglyphs and the Afterlife in Ancient Egypt*, London, BMP, 1996.

Hart, G. *A Dictionary of Egyptian Gods and Goddesses*. New York and London, Routledge, 1986.

Hart, G. *Egyptian Myths*. London, BMP, 1990.

Hornung, E., trans. E. Bredeck. *Idea into Image: Essays on Ancient Egyptian Thought*. New York, Timken Publications, 1992.

Lichtheim, M. *Ancient Egyptian Literature*. Three vols., Berkeley, University of California Press, 1973, 1976, 1980.

Lurker, M. *The Gods and Symbols of Ancient Egypt*. London, Thames and Hudson, 1980.

Parkinson, R.B. *Voices from Ancient Egypt: An Anthology of Middle Kingdom Writings*. London, BMP, 1991.

Pinch, G. *Magic in Ancient Egypt*. London, BMP, 1994.

Quirke, S. *Ancient Egyptian Religion*. London, BMP, 1992.

Roberts, A. *Hathor Rising: Serpent Power in Ancient Egypt*. Totnes, England, Northgate Publishers, 1995.

Roberts, A. *My Heart, My Mother: Death and Rebirth in Ancient Egypt*. Totnes, England, Northgate Publishers, 2000.

Sauneron, S. *The Priests of Ancient Egypt*. New York, Grove Press, 1980.

Shafer, B.E., ed. *Religion in Ancient Egypt: Gods, Myths and Personal Practice*. Ithaca, N.Y., Cornell University Press, 1991.

Shafer, B.E., ed. *Temples of Ancient Egypt*. New York and London, I. B. Tauris, 1998.

Shaw, I. and Nicholson, P. *The British Museum Dictionary of Ancient Egypt*. London, BMP, 1995.

Watterson, B. *The House of Horus at Edfu: Ritual in an Egyptian Temple*. Tempus Books, Stroud, England, 1998.

Wilkinson, R.H. *Reading Egyptian Art*. London, Thames and Hudson, 1992.

Note: BMP = British Museum Press

WEBSITES

ARTICLES BY THE AUTHOR:
www.bbc.co.uk/history/ancient/
egyptians/
www.guardian.co.uk/Archive/
Article/0,4273,4284671,00.html
www.guardianunlimited.co.uk/
science/story/0,3605,352411,00
.html
www.guardianunlimited.co.uk/sci-
ence/story/0,3605,347397,00.html

MUSEUMS AND ORGANIZATIONS:
American Research Center in Egypt: www.arce.org
British Museum, London: www.thebritishmuseum.ac.uk/
world/egypt/egypt.html
Egyptian Museum, Cairo: www.emuseum.gov.eg
Egyptian Tourist Authority: www.touregypt.net
Musée du Louvre, Paris: www.louvre.fr/louvrea.htm
Metropolitan Museum of Art, New York: www.metmuseum.org/
collections/department.asp? dep=10
Oriental Institute, University of Chicago: www.oi.uchicago.edu/OI
/default.html

INDEX

References to picture captions are in *italics*.

A

Abydos 93, 101
Admonitions of Ipuwer, The 99
afterlife 19, 27, 38–39, 60, 69
   see also death; underworld
Ahhotep, Queen 70
Aker *29*, 75
Akhenaten, King 48, 49, 88, 89
*akh*s 117, *125*, 132, 134
Amarna Period 24 *see also*
   Akhenaten
Amenemhat I, King 133
Amenhotep II, King 17
Amenhotep III, King 32, 37, 48,
   70, 71, 78, 80, 89, 90, 91,
   103, 106, 108
Amenhotep IV, King *see*
   Akhenaten
Amenhotep son of Hapu 96,
   107
Ammut *125*, *135*
amulets 64, 73, 119, 124, 130,
   132
Amun 14, 15, 32, *35*, 49, 72,
   75, 77
   barque 103
   central role 52–53
   cult centre 87–88, *89*
   Festival 102–103
   Great Hymn to Amun 55–57
   High Priestess of Amun 95
Amunet 15

Amun-Kematef 76
Amun-Ra 19, 51, *53*, 78
Anat 71–72, 81
ancestor worship 96
animal attributes 12, 32, 74–77
   see also individual animals
ankh 10, 48, 97, 106, 108
Anubis 60, 77, 124, *125*
Apis bull 68, 76
Apophis (Apep) 17, 44, 45, 47,
   76
Assessors of the underworld 124
Astarte 71–72, 81
astronomy 38–41, 93, 101, 107
aten (sun disc) 48, *49*
Aten (god) 24, 48–49
Atum 10–11, 16–17, 19, 26, 44,
   48
   Atum-Khepri 46
   relationship with Atum 10
   see also sun
Awibra-Hor, King *116*

B

ba (spirit) 116–117
baboons *93*, 104
Bakhu 29
balance 7, 19
Bastet 70, 71, 74, 75
Bat 68
Beautiful Festival of the Valley
   102, 134
bees 28, *36*, 37, 108
benu bird 45, 75
Bes 73, 112, *113*

birds 74
   see also individual birds
birth *see* childbirth
Book of Amduat, The 46, *105*,
   120
Book of Caverns, The 46
Book of Gates, The 46, 120,
   124
Book of Night, The 39
Book of the Dead, The 14, 26,
   35, 38, 60, *93*, 105, 117,
   119, *121*, *125*
   benu bird 45
   Confession 124, 127–129
   crocodiles 77
   Hymn to Ra 43
Book of the Earth, The 29
Book of Traversing Eternity,
   The 96
Books of Thoth 106
Bubastis 71, 74
Building Texts, The 107
bulls *53*, 68, 76–77
Buto 37

C

calendar 30, 40, 100
Cannibal Hymn, The 81
cats 44, 70, 71, 74, 75
chaos 7, 26–27, 34, 36, 40, 67,
   76, 79, 89
childbirth 32, 72–73, 76, 79,
   108, 111–112
Christianity 6–7, 63, 91
cobra 37, 75, *80*

PICTURE CREDITS

The publisher would like to thank the following individuals, museums and photographic libraries for permission to reproduce their material. Every care has been taken to trace copyright holders; however, if we have omitted anyone we apologize and will, if informed, make corrections in any future edition.

Abbreviations:

AKG, London = AKG
Art Archive, London = AA
British Museum, London = BM
Egyptian Museum, Cairo, Egypt = Cairo
Robert Harding Picture Library = RHPL

Front jacket Funerary mask of Tutankhamun. Cairo/Jürgen Liepe, Berlin; **page 1** Painted wooden coffin from Thebes of a 21st dynasty-priest. Harrogate Museums and Arts, Royal Pump Room Museum, Harrogate; **page 2** The journey of the sun (centre); a scene from *The Book of Caverns*, inscribed in the tomb of the female pharaoh Tawosret (ruled ca. 1188–1186BCE). François Guenet/AKG; **page 8** Nathan Benn/Corbis; **page 10** AA; **page 11** The Great Pyramid of Khufu (Cheops), Giza. White Star, Italy; **page 14** Kunsthistorisches Museum, Vienna/AKG; **page 15** The god Amun-Min. A painted limestone block from the funerary temple of Tuthmosis III, Western Thebes. Luxor Museum/AA/Dagli Orti; **page 16** Cairo/AKG; **page 19** The goddess Ma'at. New Kingdom, wall painting. Museo Archeologico, Naples/AKG; **page 20** The god Khnum.

New Kingdom, wall painting. Bojan Beceli/Corbis; **page 22** Joel W. Rogers/Corbis; **page 25** Wall painting of the god Shu separating Geb and Nut. Charles and Josette Lenars/Corbis; **page 26** Aegyptisches Museum, Berlin/AKG; **page 28** BM(EA6705); **page 29** Detail from Chapter 17 of *The Book of the Dead* of Ani, showing a representation of Aker as a lion over whose back the sun rises daily. BM (EA10470/7); **page 30** The god Hapi with a sacred offering of food representing the bounty of Egypt. A painted relief from the temple of Ramses II, Abydos. S. Purdy Matthews/Stone, London; **page 31** BM (EA37977); **page 33** Famine Stela, Sehel Island, Aswan. Charles and Josette Lenars/Corbis; **page 35** Ramses II, wearing the double crown of Upper and Lower Egypt, receives the breath of life from the god Amun. Louvre, Paris/Jacqueline Hyde/AA; **page 36** Michael Holford/BM; **page 37** The gold funerary mask of Tutankhamun. Cairo/Jürgen Liepe, Berlin; **page 40** AKG/BM; **page 41** Water deities making offerings of stars. A relief at the temple of Ramses II, Abydos. Roger Wood/Corbis; **page 42** Painted relief of the sacred barque of the sun god (centre), from the tomb of Ramses IX, Western Thebes. AA/Dagli Orti; **page 44** Philip Craven/RHPL, London; **page 45** The barque of the sun god, who is represented as the *benu* bird. Wall painting in the tomb of Sennedjem, Deir el-Medina, Thebes, 19th Dynasty. AA/Dagli Orti; **page 46** Scarab

amulet. Cairo/Jürgen Liepe, Berlin; **page 49** Kunsthistorisches Museum, Vienna/AKG; **page 50** The pyramids of Giza. Larry Lee/Corbis; **page 52** Avenue of ram-headed sphinxes, Karnak. Ludovic Maisant/Corbis; **page 53** Werner Forman Archives; **page 54** Statuette of the god Amun protecting Tutankhamun, 18th Dynasty. Louvre, Paris/Hervé Lewandowski; **page 58** AA/Dagli Orti; **page 60** Aegyptisches Museum, Berlin/AKG/Erich Lessing; **page 65** Cairo/AA/Dagli Orti; **page 66** AA/Dagli Orti; **page 67** Horus and Seth tying a knot symbolizing union of the two kingdoms of Upper and Lower Egypt. Relief on a plinth at the funerary temple of Sesostris I, el-Lisht. Cairo/AA/Dagli Orti; **page 68** Cairo/Jürgen Liepe, Berlin; **page 69** Cairo/AA/Dagli Orti; **page 70** Red granite lion, originally from the temple built by Amenhotep III at Soleb, Upper Nubia (Sudan). BM (EA2); **page 71** Cairo/AA/Dagli Orti; **page 72** Cairo/Jürgen Liepe, Berlin; **page 73** Stone slab of the Greco-Roman period showing a woman giving birth kneeling on two bricks. BM (EA61062); **page 74** Late Period figure of a cat, representing the goddess Bastet. Bronze inlaid with gold and silver. BM (EA64391); **page 75** Ludovic Maisant/Corbis; **page 76** Louvre/AA/Dagli Orti; **page 77** Mummified baby crocodile. Greco-Roman period. Cairo/Jürgen Liepe, Berlin; **page 78** BM (EA30448); **page 79** Painting from the tomb of Tuthmosis III, Western Thebes, showing the king suckled by the goddess Isis, who appears in the form of a sycamore tree. AA/Dagli Orti; **page 80** Cairo/AA/Dagli Orti; **page 81** Statue of King Horemheb protected by the god Amun. Luxor Museum/Sylvain Granadam/RHPL; **page 82** Roman-period relief at the temple of Hathor, Dendera, showing the pharaoh (the Roman emperor) making an offering to the goddess. AA/Dagli Orti; **page 84** Pylon gate at Medinet Habu. Getty/Telegraph Colour Library; **page 86** Schuster/RHPL; **page 87** Karnak temple. John Hannaford/John Warburton-Lee; **page 88** Tutankhamun and Ankhesenamun, his wife, from the reverse of his throne. Cairo/AA/Dagli Orti; **page 89** AA/Dagli Orti; **page 90** R. Ashworth/ RHPL; **page 92** A 21st-Dynasty bronze figurine of a praying priest. Louvre/AA; **page 93** Kunsthistorisches Museum, Vienna/AKG/Lessing; **page 94** AA/Dagli Orti; **page 95** Wooden statuette of the senior priestess Tuya. The mother of Amenhotep III's consort, Queen Tiye, Tuya wears a *menat* necklace with counterpoise as the symbol of her sacred office. Louvre/Bridgeman Art Library; **page 96** BM (EA1198);

page 97 Relief of Sesostris I running as part of the *sed* festival. Petrie Museum/University College, London; **page 98** Servants making offering to Prince Rahotep and Princess Nofret, from the tomb of Rahotep, Meidum. Fourth Dynasty. Cairo/AA/Dagli Orti; **page 101** Cairo/Jürgen Liepe, Berlin; **page 102** BM (EA36310); **page 103** The sacred barque of Amun-Ra. A relief from a temple of Seti I. Devizes Museum, England/AA/Eileen Tweedy; **page 104** BM (EA38); **page 105** Papyrus from reign of Tuthmosis III. AA/Dagli Orti; **page 107** Seated scribe, Fifth Dynasty. Roger Wood/Corbis; **page 108** Cairo/AA//Dagli Orti; **page 110** Louvre/Hervé Lewandowski; **page 111** *The Dream Book*, a hieratic papyrus from Deir el-Medina, Western Thebes. Reign of Ramses II. BM (EA10683); **page 113** Louvre/Bridgeman Art Library; **page 114** Robert Mertens/Photonica, London; **page 116** Cairo/Jürgen Liepe, Berlin; **page 117** Extract from the *Coffin Texts*. Cairo/Jürgen Liepe, Berlin; **page 118** Bridgeman Art Library; **page 119** Gilded cartonnage funerary mask that adorned

the mummy of an unknown woman, probably a princess. Middle Kingdom, ca. 1900BCE. BM (EA29770)/ AA/Dagli Orti; **page 120** Turtle-headed demon, a watery messenger of Osiris, from a royal tomb in the Valley of the Kings. BM (EA50704); **page 121** BM (EA10470)/AKG; **page 122** Rijksmuseum, Leiden, The Netherlands; **page 125** Cairo Museum, Egypt/AA; **page 126** Following the successful weighing of his heart, the deceased, a man called Hunefer (left), is led before Osiris by Horus. Detail from *The Book of the Dead* of Hunefer; 19th Dynasty, ca. 1290BCE. BM (EA9901)/AA; **page 130** Votive tunic with the image of the goddess Hathor, perhaps the funerary dress of a child. BM (EA43071); **page 132** Vignette from *The Book of the Dead* of Nedjemet showing the deceased tending cattle. Louvre/AA/Eileen Tweedy; **page 134** Cairo/AA/ Dagli Orti; **page 135** Detail from *The Book of the Dead* of Nebked showing Ammut, the "Devourer of the Dead", the hybrid monster that devours the hearts of those who fail the judgment before Osiris. Louvre/Werner Forman Archive.